United States Department of Agriculture

# Evaluation of Wood Species and Preservatives for Use in Wisconsin Highway Sign Posts

Stan T. Lebow
Robert J. Ross
Samuel L. Zelinka

Forest
Service

Forest Products
Laboratory

General Technical Report
FPL–GTR–231

July
2014

In cooperation with the Wisconsin Department of Transportation.

## Abstract

The Wisconsin Department of Transportation (WisDOT) uses wooden posts to support many types of signs along state highways. WisDOT currently uses red pine or Southern Pine posts treated with chromated copper arsenate (CCA) and has generally experienced satisfactory performance and service life. However, there are some areas of concern, as well as potential opportunities for diversifying the wood species and preservatives used. Warp is sometimes a problem with the current pine posts, and increased use of locally sourced wood species for the sign posts could decrease transportation costs and potentially benefit Wisconsin industries. Although CCA is a highly effective preservative, it may not be the optimum treatment for alternative wood species. This study reviewed the characteristics of alternative wood species and wood preservatives and evaluated their potential for use in Wisconsin highway sign posts.

The evaluation concluded that WisDOT's current practice of using red pine or Southern Pine posts treated with CCA is logical and may be the optimum combination of wood species and preservatives currently available. Red pine and Southern Pine are readily available and relatively strong compared with many other softwood species. Red pine is also an important commercial resource for Wisconsin and the upper Midwest. Other Wisconsin species to consider include eastern white pine and soft maples. However, strength may be a concern with eastern white pine, whereas cost may be a concern with soft maples. CCA is an effective preservative, readily treats red pine and Southern Pine, and is compatible with aluminum signs. Copper naphthenate in oil solvent appears to be one of the most logical alternatives to CCA, and would be a strong candidate for treatment of hardwoods. Copper naphthenate is non-corrosive to aluminum and would avoid warp associated with re-drying after treatment with water-based preservatives. WisDOT may want to consider purchasing a small volume of copper naphthenate-treated posts to evaluate the handling characteristics of this oil-based preservative.

Keywords: wood preservatives, wood species, sign posts, highway, Wisconsin

## Acknowledgment

The authors acknowledge the valuable input received from Matt Rauch of WisDOT in refining the study problem areas, relating field experiences, and describing WisDOT practices and procedures.

June 2014

Lebow, Stan; Ross, Robert; Zelinka, Samuel. 2014. Evaluation of wood species and preservatives for use in Wisconsin highway sign posts. General Technical Report FPL-GTR-231. Madison, WI: U.S. Department of Agriculture, Forest Service, Forest Products Laboratory. 45 p.

A limited number of free copies of this publication are available to the public from the Forest Products Laboratory, One Gifford Pinchot Drive, Madison, WI 53726–2398. This publication is also available online at www.fpl.fs.fed.us. Laboratory publications are sent to hundreds of libraries in the United States and elsewhere.

The Forest Products Laboratory is maintained in cooperation with the University of Wisconsin.

# Contents

Introduction......................................................................................................................................1

    Wisconsin's Current Sign Post Standard Specifications...........................................................1

    Wood Species Considerations...................................................................................................1

    Wood Preservative Considerations ...........................................................................................2

Objectives .........................................................................................................................................2

Wood Preservative Background........................................................................................................2

    Pressure-Treatment Preservatives and Pressure-Treated Wood...............................................2

    AWPA vs ICC-ES and AASHTO Preservative Listings .........................................................3

    Evaluating Preservative Efficacy .............................................................................................3

    Role of Solvent Characteristics in Durability ..........................................................................4

    Corrosion Testing.....................................................................................................................4

    AWPA Use Category System ...................................................................................................5

Wood Preservative Characteristics...................................................................................................5

    Role of Copper in Wood Preservatives ...................................................................................5

    Current Ground-Contact Preservatives ...................................................................................6

Corrosion Aspects of Selecting Preservatives for Sign Posts .......................................................11

    Mechanism of Corrosion in Treated Wood ...........................................................................11

    Review of Corrosion Data from New Wood Preservatives ...................................................12

    Special Corrosion Considerations for Sign Posts ..................................................................14

    Corrosion Recommendations..................................................................................................14

Summary of Preservatives' Potential for Sign Post Treatments ....................................................14

    Water-Based Preservatives.....................................................................................................15

    Oil-Based Preservatives .........................................................................................................16

Wood Species Options for Wisconsin DOT Signposts ..................................................................17

    Wood Species Currently Listed in WisDOT Signpost Specifications ...................................17

    Hem-Fir...................................................................................................................................21

    Treatability and Durability of Other Wisconsin Wood Species ............................................23

    Ash..........................................................................................................................................23

    Aspen......................................................................................................................................24

    Balsam Fir...............................................................................................................................24

    Basswood ...............................................................................................................................25

    Birch—Paper and Yellow.......................................................................................................25

    Eastern Hemlock.....................................................................................................................26

    Elm..........................................................................................................................................27

    Maples, Hard...........................................................................................................................27

    Maples, Soft............................................................................................................................28

    Spruce.....................................................................................................................................28

Engineering Properties of Wisconsin Wood Species .....................................................................29

    Common Mechanical Properties.............................................................................................29

    Moisture Content and Shrinkage ...........................................................................................30

    Minimizing Warp in Sign Posts .............................................................................................32

Other Options: Structural Wood Composites and Naturally Durable Species................................34

    Structural Wood Composites ..................................................................................................34

    Naturally Durable Species ......................................................................................................35

Summary of Potential Use of Wisconsin Species in Sign Posts ....................................................35

Wooden Signage Post Specifications in Other States ....................................................................36

    Wood Species Referenced by Other States ............................................................................38

    Wood Preservatives Referenced by Other States ..................................................................39

Summary .........................................................................................................................................40

    Preservatives and Wood Species ...........................................................................................40

References........................................................................................................................................42

# Evaluation of Wood Species and Preservatives for Use in Wisconsin Highway Sign Posts

**Stan T. Lebow,** Research Forest Products Technologist
**Robert J. Ross,** Supervisory Research General Engineer
**Sameul L. Zelinka,** Research Materials Engineer

Forest Products Laboratory, Madison, Wisconsin

## Introduction

The Wisconsin Department of Transportation (WisDOT) administers approximately 11,800 miles (18,990 km) of state highways (WisDOT 2014). WisDOT uses preservative-treated wood posts for much of the signage along these highways because wood is relatively inexpensive, easy to install, and has the necessary strength properties to tolerate typical Wisconsin wind loads. Although WisDOT's experience with wood sign posts has been generally positive, there are some areas of concern, as well as potential opportunities for diversifying the wood species and preservatives used. WisDOT and the USDA Forest Products Laboratory conducted a comprehensive literature review to examine those concerns and
opportunities.

## Wisconsin's Current Sign Post Standard Specifications

Wood sign posts are covered under WisDOT Section 634 Wood and Tubular Steel Sign Posts, but with reference to conformance to Section 507.2.2 Lumber and Timber (for grading), Section 507.2.2.6 Preservative Treatments (for preservative criteria), and Section 614.2.5 Wood Posts and Offset Blocks (for species selection and wood quality). However, Section 634 additionally specifies that wood sign posts will be either beam and stringer grade or structural joist and plank grade material with a minimum stress grade rating of 1200 $f_b$ (1200 lb/in$^2$ fiber stress in bending) at 19% maximum moisture content (MC). Section 634 also limits the choice of preservative treatments to chromated copper arsenate from the Section 507.2.2.6 listing that also includes creosote, pentachlorophenol, copper naphthenate (both oil and water-based), ammoniacal copper zinc arsenate (ACZA), ammoniacal copper quat (ACQ types A or B), and copper azole (types A or B). Section 507.2.2.6 specifies that the wood be treated to meet the penetration and retention requirements of American Wood Protection Association Use Category 4A (general use ground contact) and this specification is not amended by Section 634. Section 634 also does not amend the wood species listed in Section 614.2.5, thus allowing use of Douglas-fir, Southern Pine, ponderosa pine,

jack pine, white pine, red pine, western hemlock, western larch, Hem-Fir species, and oak species. However, discussion with WisDOT personnel indicates that oaks will be removed from the species listed. The net effect of the WisDOT specifications is to provide sign posts with the following characteristics:

- Wood quality: Beam and stringer grade or structural joist and plank grade with minimum fiber stress in bending ($f_b$) of 1,200 lb/in$^2$.

- Wood species: Douglas-fir, Southern Pine, ponderosa pine, jack pine, white pine, red pine, western hemlock, western larch, and Hem-Fir (species grouping).

- Preservative treatment: Chromated copper arsenate to meet AWPA Use Category 4A (6.4 kg/m$^3$ or 0.4 lb/ft$^3$) retention.

## Wood Species Considerations

Use of locally sourced wood for the sign posts decreases transportation costs and potentially benefits Wisconsin industries. Currently, red pine is the preferred wood species because it is locally grown and locally treated, but Southern Pine posts are also used when there is an insufficient supply of red pine. Southern Pine is easily treated with wood preservatives and readily available but is primarily grown in the southeastern United States. Possible alternative species include those currently allowed under WisDOT specifications (Douglas-fir, jack pine, white pine, and oak) as well as other softwood and hardwood species that occur commonly in Wisconsin. However, some of these species may not be locally available in sufficient quantity, while others may not grow to sufficient size, have sufficient strength (Kretschmann 2010), or be treatable with preservatives (Smith 1986; Gjovik and Schumann 1992). Some Wisconsin wood species have a degree of natural durability (Clausen 2010), although it is not clear that this durability is sufficient for use in sign post applications.

An acceptable wood species also must not exhibit excessive warp during drying or while in service. In part because of their length (up to 6.7 m (22 ft)), the red pine and Southern Pine sign posts are vulnerable to twisting or warping as they dry following treatment. Current WisDOT practice is to have the posts stickered after treatment to promote drying and to minimize the time that the posts are exposed horizontally outdoors during storage. An alternative approach is to close-stack the posts after treatment to minimize drying and warp prior to installation. However, this approach raises the concern that drying and warp might occur after installation and compromise the appearance or function of the sign.

## Wood Preservative Considerations

Most Wisconsin wood species do not have sufficient natural durability to be used in direct contact with soil. To provide the necessary durability, the wood must be pressure-treated with preservatives that are toxic to wood-decaying fungi. Currently, WisDOT is specifying that posts be treated with chromated copper arsenate (CCA). CCA is an effective and inexpensive preservative that has been widely used for treatment of wooden construction materials for decades. However, CCA is considered a Restricted Use Pesticide (RUP) by the U.S. Environmental Protection Agency (EPA), and it is possible that it will no longer be available sometime in the future. It is also difficult to penetrate some wood species with CCA during the treatment process.

In the past decade, numerous alternatives to CCA have been developed, and some have gained substantial market share (Lebow 2010). The most readily available of these are water-based formulations that rely primarily on copper for protection against decay and termite attack. In addition, some of the most recent copper-based formulations would reportedly need to be modified to penetrate red pine or other Wisconsin species (McIntyre 2010). Research also suggests that water-based copper formulations are not as effective in protecting hardwoods (Lebow et al. 2010). Copper-free water-based formulations have also been developed but may not have sufficient durability to protect wood placed directly in contact with the ground. Oil-based preservatives such as copper naphthenate are another option, but oil-based preservatives can have odor and surface characteristics that are sometimes considered undesirable.

Compatibility with aluminum signs is an important consideration for alternative preservative treatments. WisDOT conducted a trial with one of these copper-based formulations (ACQ) and found that the preservative caused corrosion of the aluminum sign (Wilson 2004). Manufacturers of other copper-based preservative formulations claim the treated wood can be placed in contact with aluminum, but there is little research available on their compatibility with aluminum signs. WisDOT currently attaches aluminum signs to CCA-treated posts with galvanized lag screws. When ACQ-treated sign posts were evaluated, excessive corrosion of the aluminum occurred around the bolt-hole (Wilson 2004). While not specifically mentioned in the WisDOT report, the photographs in the report suggest that a galvanic couple was occurring between the galvanized lag screw and the aluminum sign. Galvanic corrosion occurs when dissimilar metals

are electrically connected in a wet environment; the more anodic metal corrodes at a faster rate than it would if exposed by itself and the cathodic metal corrodes more slowly. Which metal acts as the anode/cathode depends on the metals and the environment. In seawater, aluminum is slightly cathodic to zinc. However, the photographs from the preliminary corrosion investigation (Wilson 2004) suggest that the aluminum sign is acting as the anode and preferentially corroding in the vicinity of the zinc-plated lagscrew.

The use of alternative wood preservatives presents two possibilities for increased corrosion of aluminum signs: (1) increased general corrosion of the aluminum sign and/or zinc-plated fastener (2) increased galvanic corrosion in the new environment. If the majority of the increased corrosion is caused by galvanic corrosion, placing a nylon washer between the lag screw and aluminum sign should greatly reduce the observed corrosion.

# Objectives

The objectives of this project were as follows:

- Review properties of wood preservatives and evaluate their potential for use in treatment of sign posts manufactured from Wisconsin wood species.

- Review properties of Wisconsin wood species and evaluate their potential for use in sign post applications.

- Review current WisDOT post storage practices and recommend options for minimizing warp during storage and use.

# Wood Preservative Background

When considered in its broadest context, a wood preservative is any substance or material that, when applied to wood, extends the useful service life of the wood product. In more practical terms, wood preservatives are generally chemicals that are either toxic to wood-degrading organisms or cause some change in wood properties that renders the wood less vulnerable to degradation, or both. Most wood preservatives contain pesticide ingredients, and as such must have registration with the U.S. Environmental Protection Agency (EPA). However, some preservatives such as those based on water repellents, work on the basis of moisture exclusion and do not contain pesticides. Preservatives that do contain pesticides are required to provide information on the type and concentration of pesticide on the label. Because the term "wood preservative" is applied to a broad range of products, there is often confusion or misunderstanding about the types of products being described, and some degree of specificity is needed.

## Pressure-Treatment Preservatives and Pressure-Treated Wood

The greatest volume of wood preservatives is used in the pressure treatment of wood at specialized treatment facilities. In these treatment plants, bundles of wood products are placed into large pressure cylinders and combinations of vacuum, pressure, and sometimes heat are used to force the preservative deeply into the wood. Pressure-treated wood and the pressure-treatment preservatives differ from non-pressure preservatives in three important ways. (1) Pressure-treated wood has much deeper and more uniform preservative penetration than wood treated in other manners. (2) Most preservatives used in pressure treatment are not available for application by the public. (3) Pressure-treatment preservatives and pressure-treated wood undergo review by standard-setting organizations to ensure that the resulting product will be sufficiently durable in the intended end-use. Standards also apply to treatment processes and require specific quality control and quality assurance procedures for the treated wood product. This level of oversight is needed because pressure-treated wood is used in applications where it is expected to provide service for decades, and where premature failure could result in injury or death. In contrast, non-pressure preservatives may undergo relatively little review, other than the EPA evaluation of pesticide toxicity.

Preservatives have a range of properties that may make them more or less suitable for treatment of signposts. The most important of these is their efficacy in protecting the wood from attack by decay fungi and insects. EPA registration status and the accompanying allowable uses on the EPA label are also critical, but current EPA labeling puts few limitations on use of labeled preservatives for highway applications. Because the signage posts are typically in direct contact with aluminum signs, corrosiveness of the treated wood is also important. Other characteristics such as toxicity, odor, and surface cleanliness may also be considered, although these properties are less important for signage posts than for applications where human contact is more frequent. And finally, the preservative must be commercially available or have the likelihood of becoming available in the future. This last consideration is particularly relevant for pressure-treatment preservatives because conversion of a pressure-treatment facility to alternative preservatives is an expensive process that is unlikely to be undertaken without some assurance of a sustained and profitable market for the treated product.

## AWPA vs ICC-ES and AASHTO Preservative Listings

Before a wood preservative can be approved for pressure treatment of structural members, it must be evaluated to ensure that it provides the necessary durability and that it does not greatly reduce the strength properties of the wood. The EPA typically does not evaluate how well a wood preservative protects the wood. Traditionally this evaluation has been conducted through the standardization process of the American Wood Protection Association (AWPA). The AWPA Book of Standards lists a series of laboratory and field exposure tests that must be conducted when evaluating new wood preservatives. The durability of test products is compared with that of established durable products and nondurable controls. The results of those tests are then presented to the appropriate AWPA subcommittees for review. AWPA subcommittees are composed of representatives from industry, academia, and government agencies who have familiarity with conducting and interpreting durability evaluations. Preservative standardization by AWPA is a two-step process. If the performance of a new preservative is considered appropriate, it is first listed as a potential preservative. Secondary committee action is needed to have the new preservative listed for specific commodities and to set the required treatment level.

More recently the International Code Council–Evaluation Service (ICC–ES) has evolved as an additional route for gaining building code acceptance of new types of pressure-treated wood. In contrast to AWPA, the ICC–ES does not standardize preservatives. Instead, it issues evaluation reports that provide evidence that a building product complies with building codes. The data and other information needed to obtain an evaluation report are first established as acceptance criteria. AC326, which sets the performance criteria used by ICC–ES to evaluate proprietary wood preservatives, and requires submittal of documentation from accredited third party agencies in accordance with AWPA, ASTM, and EN standard test methods. The results of those tests are then reviewed by an evaluation committee to determine if the preservative has met the appropriate acceptance criteria.

The American Association of State Highway and Transportation Officials (AASHTO) also has a standard specification for Preservatives and Pressure Treatment Processes for Timber (AASHTO M 133). This specification is under the oversight of AASHTO Technical Section 4c–Coatings, Paints, Preservatives, Bonding Agents, and Traffic Markings. Unlike AWPA and ICC-ES, AASHTO does not evaluate new preservatives for inclusion in AASHTO M 133. Instead, AASHTO lists some (but not necessarily all) preservatives that have been either standardized by AWPA or have an ICC-ES evaluation report. AASHTO M 133 also refers to AWPA standards or ICC-ES Evaluation Reports for specifications on treatment processes and limitations.

## Evaluating Preservative Efficacy

Evaluating preservative efficacy and judging its expected durability for sign posts is not an exact science. Wood preservative efficacy is evaluated using a variety of laboratory and field exposures, and the applicability of these test results to real world durability depends on how well the test simulates in-service conditions. Ideally, a preservative would be tested under identical conditions to those in service, but this can become impractical for products expected to remain durable for many years or even many decades. In general, the shorter and more artificial the test conditions, the less confidence it provides for in-service performance. Although relatively short laboratory tests can be useful indicators in comparison with more established preservatives systems, these tests should not be viewed as absolute evidence of future performance. They may however, provide insight into a preservatives' potential vulnerability or resistance to a certain type of organism. The type and severity of tests depends somewhat on the intended end-use of the treated wood. Wood intended for use in ground-contact applications (i.e., sign posts, piles, poles) is generally subjected to the most severe tests, which include multiple years of in-ground exposure.

## Stake and Post Field Tests

Ground-contact tests with stakes or posts are the most traditional and typically the most severe (other than marine exposure) method of evaluating preservatives. They are also the most appropriate methods for evaluating preservatives to be used in signage posts. In these tests, specimens ranging from thin strips to full-size posts are partially buried and then periodically inspected (AWPA Methods E7 and E8) (AWPA 2012). Inspections are typically visual ratings based on a scale of 10, 9, 8, 7, 6, 4, and 0 with 10 representing no deterioration and 0 representing failure. Prior to 1993, many researchers, including those at the FPL, used a 5-scale rating that does not exactly transfer to the ratings used since that time. Because of this discrepancy, the durability of FPL's older "2 by 4" (38 by 89 mm) stake data will be presented in terms of percentage failures or average years to failure (Woodward et al. 2011). "Push" or "pull" tests have also been widely used for posts that are too large to remove from the ground. In a push or pull test, a set force is applied to the top of the post and it is given a "pass" rating if it does not snap at the groundline. Although "2 by 4" sized stakes were often used in the past, the most common specimen dimension over the last two decades has been the smaller 19- by 19- by 457-mm (¾- by ¾- by 18-in.) stake. The smaller stakes typically fail more rapidly than larger stakes and are assumed to "accelerate" testing relative to specimens with larger dimensions or to in-service materials. The assumption of test acceleration has been used to justify shortening test durations in evaluating new preservatives to as little as 3 years. However, the assumption is somewhat murky because the relationship between time to decay in "2 by 4" and 19- by 19- by 457-mm (¾- by ¾- by 18-in.) stakes is highly variable. Deterioration is more rapid in warm moist climates than in cool or dry climates, and warmer climates also ensure termite activity, whereas termites may not be present in more northern locations. Soil properties also play a role with decay appearing to progress more rapidly in highly organic soils and more slowly in more compacted soils. The presence and extent of copper-tolerant fungi in the soil also varies within and between test sites.

## Role of Solvent Characteristics in Durability

Many preservatives have been formulated for use as either an oil-based or water-based treatment. Differences in wood durability can be present depending on whether the preservative is carried in oil or water. Also, multiple types of oil-based solvents are used in wood preservative formulations, but for the purposes of this discussion we can group them into two categories: "light" and "heavy" oils. Light solvents (such as mineral spirits) have a lower viscosity and higher volatility. Heavier oils (such as diesel) have higher viscosity and lower volatility and remain in the treated product for many years. Preservative treatments in heavy solvents are usually more durable than those in light solvents because the solvent itself acts as a preservative. Diesel alone has been shown to extend the life of 2 by 4 stakes by many years (Woodward et al. 2011). When reviewing efficacy data between oil-based systems, it is important to consider the type of solvent used. Similarly, a preservative formulation applied with a heavy oil solvent will be more durable than one applied as a water-based formulation. There is less difference in durability between formulations applied using water or light solvent because the light solvent does vaporize from the wood. However, the light solvent treatment may have advantages in increased penetration and more uniform distribution of the active ingredient within the wood structure. This may be especially true for water-based treatments that are dispersions or emulsions rather than true solutions.

## Corrosion Testing

Corrosion testing was often an afterthought in evaluating wood preservatives, but has grown in importance with the increased use of copper-based preservatives. AWPA has methods for evaluating corrosiveness of preservative treatment solutions to metal treating equipment (AWPA Method E17) and for evaluating the corrosiveness of the treated wood to metal fasteners (AWPA Method E12). In the treatment solution method, metal coupons (typically 25 by 51 by 2 mm (1 by 2 by 1/16 in.)) are weighed and suspended in the preservative and agitated. The test is continued for 25 days with frequent replacement of the treatment solution. At the end of the test, the coupon is cleaned and re-weighed to determine weight loss from corrosion. Water and a known preservative solution are evaluated for comparison.

To evaluate the corrosiveness of the treated wood, metal coupons (typically 15 by 51 mm (1 by 2 in.)) are placed between two blocks of treated wood, and nylon bolts joining the two wood blocks are tightened to ensure good contact between the wood and metal. These assemblies are then placed into a room maintained at 122 °F (50 °C) and 90% RH for 366 to 720 h. Extent of corrosion (mils per year) is calculated by dividing the weight loss by the surface area, metal density, and by the duration of the test. Untreated wood and wood treated with a known preservative are tested for comparison. Both methods, and particularly the treated wood method, have been a source of concern because of the poor correlation to observed in-service corrosion.

Table 1. AWPA or ICC-ES-ESR retentions (kg/m$^3$) for preservatives used in ground contact. Retentions are for Southern Pine and red pine species; retentions for other softwoods are generally similar, but not all softwoods are listed for all preservatives. NL is not listed.

| Preservative | Listed in AASHTO M 133 | Sawn lumber/Timbers | | | Posts | | Utility poles | | | Piling |
|---|---|---|---|---|---|---|---|---|---|---|
| | | UC4A | UC4B | UC4C | UC4A | UC4B | UC4A | UC4B | UC4C | UC4C |
| Water-based | | | | | | | | | | |
| ACC | X | 8.0 | NL | NL | 8.0 | NL | NL | NL | NL | NL |
| ACQ-A | | 6.4 | NL | NL | NL | NL | NL | NL | NL | NL |
| ACQ-B | X | 6.4 | 9.6 | 9.6 | 6.4 | 8.0 | 9.6 | 9.6 | 9.6 | NL |
| ACQ-C | X | 6.4 | 9.6 | 9.6 | 6.4 | 8.0 | NL | NL | NL | 12.8 |
| ACQ-D | X | 6.4 | 9.6 | 9.6 | 6.4 | 8.0 | NL | NL | NL | NL |
| ACZA | X | 6.4 | 9.6 | 9.6 | 6.4 | 8.0 | 9.6 | 9.6 | 9.6 | 12.8 |
| CA-B | X | 3.3 | 5.0 | 5.0 | 3.3 | 4.0 | 5.0 | 5.0 | 5.0 | 6.6 |
| CA-C | X | 2.4 | 5.0 | 5.0 | 2.4 | 4.0 | 5.0 | 5.0 | 5.0 | 6.6 |
| CCA-C | X | 6.4 | 9.6 | 9.6 | 6.4 | 8.0 | 9.6 | 9.6 | 9.6 | 12.8 |
| CDDC | | 3.2 | NL | NL | NL | NL | NL | NL | NL | NL |
| CuN-W (copper naph) | | 1.76 | NL | NL | 1.76 | NL | NL | NL | NL | NL |
| KDS | | 7.5 | NL | NL | 7.5 | NL | NL | NL | NL | NL |
| ESR-1721 $u$CA-B | X | 2.4 | 3.7 | 5.3 | 2.4 | 3.7 | 2.4 | 3.7 | 5.3 | 5.3 |
| ESR-1721 $u$CA-C | X | 2.4 | 3.7 | 5.3 | 2.4 | 3.7 | 2.4 | 3.7 | 5.3 | 5.3 |
| ESR-1980 | X | 5.4 | 9.6 | NL | 5.4 | 9.6 | 5.4 | 9.6 | NL | NL |
| ESR-2240 | X | 2.4 | 3.7 | NL | 2.4 | 3.7 | 2.4 | 3.7 | NL | NL |
| Oil-based | | | | | | | | | | |
| Creosote | X | 160 | 160 | 192 | 128 | 160 | 96 | 120 | 144 | 192 |
| PCP (pentachlorophenol) | X | 8.0 | 8.0 | 8.0 | 6.4 | 8.0 | 4.8 | 6.1 | 7.2 | 9.6 |
| CuN (copper naph) | X | 0.96 | 1.2 | 1.2 | 0.88 | 1.1 | 0.96 | 1.28 | 2.1 | 1.6 |

[a]ICC-ES preservatives are not specifically listed by use categories. Listings in this table are based on example applications provided in ESR reports.

## AWPA Use Category System

The type of preservative applied is often dependent on the requirements of the specific application. For example, direct contact with soil or water is considered a severe deterioration hazard and preservatives used in these applications must have a high degree of leach resistance and efficacy against a broad spectrum of organisms. These same preservatives may also be used at lower retentions to protect wood exposed in lower deterioration hazards, such as above the ground. The exposure is less severe for wood that is partially protected from the weather and preservatives that lack the permanence or toxicity to withstand continued exposure to precipitation, but may be effective in those applications. Other formulations may be so readily leachable that they can only be used indoors.

To guide selection of the types of preservatives and loadings appropriate to a specific end-use, the AWPA developed Use Category System (UCS) standards. The UCS standards simplify the process of finding appropriate preservatives and preservative retentions for specific end uses. They categorize treated wood applications by the severity of the deterioration hazard, as well as the structural significance of the application. The lowest category, Use Category 1 (UC1) is for wood that is used in interior construction and kept dry, while UC2 is for interior wood, completely protected from the weather but occasionally damp. UC3 is for exterior wood used above ground, while UC4 is for wood used in ground contact in exterior applications. UC5 includes applications that place treated wood in contact with seawater and marine borers. Individual commodity specifications then list all the preservatives that are standardized for a specific Use Category, as well as the appropriate preservative retention.

One of the disadvantages of the Use Category System is that there is no longer a separate standard specifically for wood used in highway construction. Wood used in highway construction is typically considered to fall into UC4A, B, or C, depending on whether the wood is used above ground or in ground contact, as well as its structural significance. Because signage posts are placed into contact with the ground, but are not considered structurally critical (in comparison to guardrail posts, for example), they have typically been considered a UC4A application. In contrast, guardrail posts are classified as a UC4B application. For most preservative systems, the only difference between UC4A and UC4B is an increase in the required retention (Table 1). However, a few preservatives standardized for UC4A are not standardized for UC4B.

# Wood Preservative Characteristics

## Role of Copper in Wood Preservatives

Copper has been used in wood preservatives for centuries and remains a common component in current formulations. It is effective against most types of decay fungi as well as major insect pests. Unlike carbon-based preservatives, copper is not biodegraded and retains its efficacy for long periods. However, copper does have some disadvantages and limitations. Although it is not biodegraded, it is somewhat leachable and thus the reservoir of available preservative is slowly depleted over time. The importance of leaching in long-term efficacy depends on the copper concentration, preservative formulation, and distribution of copper within the treated material. Copper is also not effective against all types of fungi. Some mold/stain fungi can grow on copper-treated wood, and certain types of decay fungi are classified as "copper-tolerant." These fungi can sporadically cause severe and rapid damage in wood treated with copper, and thus commercial copper-based preservatives typically include a co-biocide (i.e., arsenic, quaternary ammonium compounds, triazoles, naphthenic acids) to provide additional protection. A third and highly relevant limitation of copper-based preservatives is their potential corrosiveness to various metals, including (in some cases) aluminum. The extent of corrosion is dependent on the preservative formulation and the resulting concentration of free, water-soluble copper ions. Typically, water-based formulations are more corrosive than oil-based formulations, and water-based formulations without chromium are more corrosive than those with chromium. Other additives (such as borates) are also used to lessen corrosion.

Historically, most copper-based wood preservatives have used copper that is solubilized in water, although there are two notable exceptions (copper naphthenate and copper-8-quinolinolate). Copper metal and copper oxides and carbonates have relatively low water solubility, but copper solubility can be greatly increased with use of acidic or alkaline solutions. Soluble copper salts such as copper sulfate have also been used, but these formulations tend to be more corrosive and leachable because more copper remains soluble within the treated wood. As a result, current commercial formulations use either acidic solutions (chromated copper arsenate, acid copper chromate) or alkaline solutions that rely on either ammonia (ACQ type B, ACZA) or ethanolamine (i.e., ACQ types A, D, and C, copper azole, KDS, water-based copper naphthenate) compounds to solubilize the copper. (Note: that A, B, C, and D designations for ACQ refer to the order in which they were listed in AWPA Standards). Once the wood has been treated and allowed to dry, the copper becomes much less soluble because the pH becomes more neutral and because a portion of the copper undergoes ion-exchange reactions with the wood substrate. In the case of the ammoniacal formulations, the volatilization of the ammonia during drying also results in copper precipitates within the wood structure. It is important to note, however, that small amounts of copper remain slightly soluble and are gradually solubilized over time. Although relatively slight, this solubility allows copper to leach from the wood and also to potentially corrode metal in contact with the wood. The chromium in the acidic chromated

copper arsenate and acid copper chromate formulations helps to mitigate this corrosion, but wood treated with the alkaline formulations remains somewhat more corrosive than untreated wood. Because the treatment solutions contain a much greater concentration of soluble copper ions than the treated wood, chromium-free copper solutions tend to be substantially more corrosive than the wood itself. This effect can be observed when fasteners are installed in pressure-treated wood before it has dried following treatment.

In recent years, a different approach to formulating copper-based preservatives has become widely used. In these formulations, the copper is not solubilized. Instead, copper carbonate is mechanically milled to very small particles (generally less than 1 micron in diameter) and suspended in the treating solution. These particulate formulations appear to have several advantages, including potentially less corrosiveness because of lower concentrations of soluble copper ions in the treatment solution and treated wood. Copper in these formulations is also reported to be less leachable from the treated product, and cost savings are achieved by not depending on the relatively expensive ethanolamine used in the soluble copper preservatives. Wood treated with the particulate copper formulations also has less coloration than wood treated with soluble copper formulations, but this characteristic may not be of importance in treating sign posts. A potential disadvantage of the particulate copper preservatives is that they may not penetrate as deeply or uniformly into the wood substrate as the soluble copper preservatives. They are primarily used for treatment of Southern Pine species, which are readily penetrated with preservatives and have pore sizes that allow the particles to move into the wood. Currently, none of these particulate copper formulations have been evaluated or standardized by the AWPA. However, several formulations do have ICC-ES Evaluation Reports and have also been included in AASTHTO M 133.

## Current Ground-Contact Preservatives

A number of preservatives are currently listed for treatment of wood to be used in contact with the ground, either through AWPA standards or ICC-ES evaluation reports (Table 1). Most (but not all) of these preservatives are also listed in AASHTO M 133. The preservative retentions vary by Use Category, and type of commodity. In this section, the properties of the preservatives listed in Table 1 are summarized below in alphabetical order.

### Acid Copper Chromate (ACC)

ACC is an acidic water-based preservative that has been used in Europe and the United States since the 1920s. ACC contains 31.8% copper oxide and 68.2% chromium trioxide. The treated wood has a light greenish-brown color and little noticeable odor. ACC is applied by pressure treatment, but current use is largely limited to wood used in cooling towers. ACC is standardized by the AWPA at retentions of 4.0 kg/m$^3$ (0.25 lb/ft$^3$) for above ground use and 8.0 kg/m$^3$

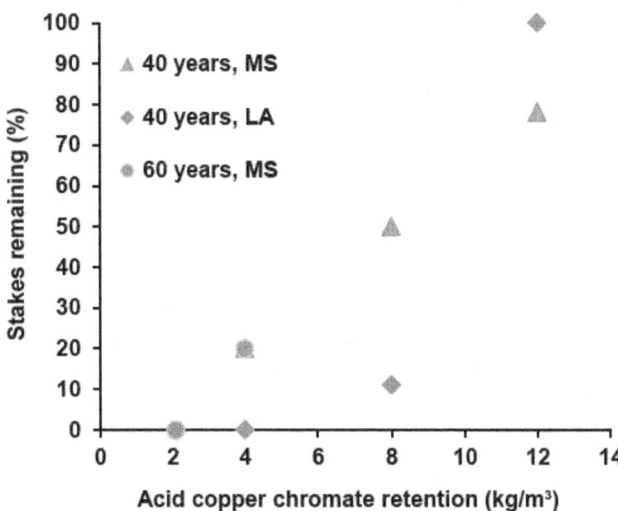

Figure 1. Durability of ACC-treated 38- by 89-mm (2- by 4-in. nominal) southern pine stakes exposed in Mississippi or Louisiana for 40 or 60 years.

(0.5 lb/ft³) in ground contact. Tests on stakes exposed to decay and termite attack indicate that wood well-impregnated with ACC gives acceptable service (Woodward et al. 2011) (Fig. 1). However, it may be susceptible to attack by some species of copper-tolerant fungi, and because of this its use is sometimes limited to above-ground applications. It may be difficult to obtain adequate penetration of ACC in some of the more difficult-to-treat wood species such as spruce or Douglas-fir. This is because ACC must be used at relatively low treating temperatures and because rapid reactions of chromium in the wood can hinder further penetration during longer pressure periods. The high chromium content of ACC, however, has the benefit of preventing much of the corrosion that might otherwise occur with an acidic copper preservative. The treatment solution does use hexavalent chromium, but the chromium is converted to the more benign trivalent state during treatment and subsequent storage of the wood. Availability of facilities pressure-treating with ACC is currently limited.

## Ammoniacal Copper Quat (ACQ-B)

ACQ formulations combine copper and quaternary ammonium compounds (quats) to protect wood from both fungal and insect attack. ACQ-B (Akaline copper quat, Type B) is the earliest ACQ formulation standardized and commercialized. Unlike the other ACQ formulations, it relies primarily on ammonium hydroxide to solubilize the copper. The actives composition of ACQ-B is 66.7% CuO and 33.3% didecyl dimethyl ammonium chloride/carbonate (DDAC). ACQ-B is currently standardized by the American Wood Protection Association (AWPA) at retentions ranging from 4.0 kg/m³ (0.25 lb/ft³) for above-ground use to 9.6 kg/m³ (0.6 lb/ft³) for critical ground-contact applications. ACQ-B

treated wood has a dark greenish-brown color that fades to a lighter brown and may have a slight ammonia odor until the wood dries. It is used primarily in the western wood United States because the ammonia helps the preservative penetrate into more difficult to treat wood species such as Douglas-fir. Like many other soluble copper preservatives, ACQ-B solution and to some extent the treated wood can be expected to increase corrosion of aluminum signs and other metal components.

## Alkaline copper quat, (ACQ Types A, D and C and ESR-1980)

ACQ Types A, D, and C use ethanolamine to solubilize the copper. Wood treated with copper ethanolamine tends to have less odor and a more uniform surface appearance than that treated with copper in ammonia, and thus is more widely used for easily treated species such as Southern Pine. ACQ-A has a higher DDAC concentration (actives ratio of 50% DDAC, 50% CuO). ACQ-C has a different form of quaternary ammonium compound (alkylbenzyl dimethyl ammonium compound) with an actives ratio of 66.7% CuO and 33.3% quat. ACQ-D is the most commonly used formulation in the eastern United States. It is similar to ACQ-B, with an actives ratio of 66.7% CuO and 33.3% DDAC, but differs in the use of ethanolamine to solubilize the copper rather than ammonia. ACQ-A, C, and D are standardized by the AWPA at retentions ranging from 2.4 kg/m³ (0.15 lb/ft³) for above-ground use to 12.8 kg/m³ (0.8 lb/ft³) for terrestrial piles. Exposure data indicate that the ethanolamine formulation of ACQ-D may not be as effective as the ammoniacal ACQ-B formulation at low concentrations, but is similarly effective at higher concentrations (Fig. 2). However, compatibility with aluminum remains a concern.

ESR-1980 is a particulate copper formulation that is produced in copper/quat ratios of 1:1 and 2:1 (analogous to the actives ratios in ACQ-A and ACQ-D). ESR-1980 has not been standardized by the AWPA, but was evaluated by the International Code Commission Evaluation Service (ICC-ES) and is included in AASHTO M 133. Its retention requirements range from 1.6 kg/m³ (0.10 lb/ft³ ) for certain above-ground applications to 9.6 kg/m³ (0.6 lb/ft³) for critical ground-contact applications. Product literature indicates that ESR-1980 may be less corrosive to aluminum and other metals than the soluble-copper formulations of ACQ. As with other particulate copper formulations, this formulation is primarily used to treat more permeable pine species.

## Ammoniacal Copper Zinc Arsenate (ACZA, Previously ACA)

ACZA is a refinement of the preservative ammoniacal copper arsenate (ACA) that had been in commercial use since the 1930s. In ACZA, a portion of the arsenic is replaced with zinc, yielding an actives ratio of copper oxide (50%), zinc oxide (25%), and arsenic pentoxide (25%). ACZA is standardized by the AWPA for a wide range of applications

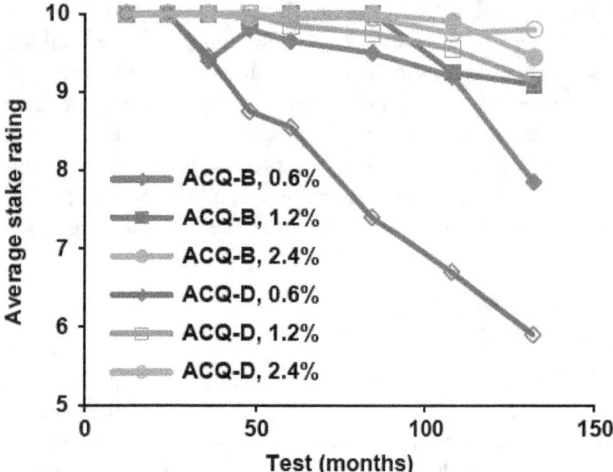

**Figure 2. Ratings of 19- by 19-mm (¾- by ¾-in.) Southern Pine stakes treated with varying solution strengths of ACQ-B or ACQ-D and exposed in southern Mississippi.**

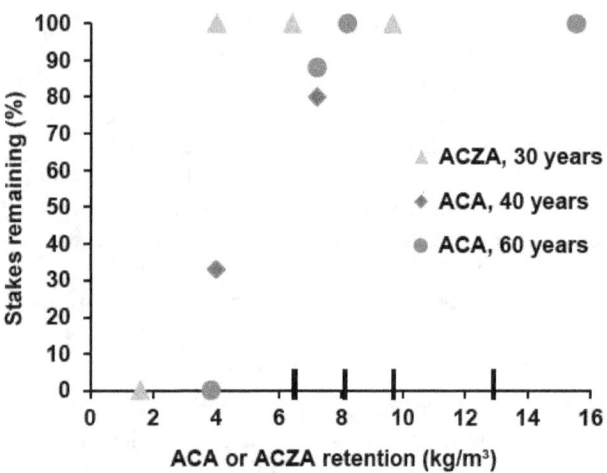

**Figure 3. Durability of 2 by 4 (nominal) Southern Pine stakes treated with ACA or ACZA and exposed in Mississipi. Soild black lines on x-axis indicate range of AWPA standard retentions for wood to be used in ground contact.**

at retentions from 4.0 kg/m³ (0.25 lb/ft³) for above-ground use to 40 kg/m³ (2.5 lb/ft³) for marine piles. It is an effective preservative (Fig. 3, Table 2) and is currently used to treat poles, piles, timbers, and other "industrial" type products that need a long service life. ACZA uses ammonia to solubilize the copper, and the wood may have a slight ammonia odor until it is thoroughly dried after treatment. The ammonia in the treating solution, in combination with processing techniques such as steaming and extended pressure periods, allow ACZA to obtain better penetration of difficult to treat wood species than many other water-based wood preservatives. Treating facilities using ACZA are primarily located in

western United States, where many of the native tree species are difficult to treat with other waterborne preservatives. As with many of the other copper-based preservatives, compatibility with aluminum is a concern. ACZA is classified as a RUP by the EPA.

## Chromated Copper Arsenate (CCA)

CCA is a water-based preservative that has been used for pressure treatment since the 1940s and was the predominant preservative in the United States from the 1970s through 2003. Since 2003, its use has been limited to non-residential applications. Three formulations (CCA-A, CCA-B, and CCA-C) have been widely used in the past, but the CCA-C formulation has been the dominant formulation for at least two decades because of its combination of efficacy and resistance to leaching. CCA-C has an actives ratio of 47.5% chromium trioxide, 18.5% copper oxide, and 34.0% arsenic pentoxide. CCA-C is standardized by the AWPA at retentions ranging from 4.0 kg/m³ (0.25 lb/ft³) for above-ground use to 40 kg/m³ (2.5 lb/ft³) for marine piles. In addition to being the most common treatment for wooden sign posts, it is still widely used for treatment of poles, piles, and timbers. CCA has decades of proven performance in field trials (Woodward et al. 2011) (Fig. 4) and in-service applications. In accelerated testing, CCA remains the "gold standard" reference preservative used to evaluate the performance of other waterborne wood preservatives. Like ACC, CCA may have difficulty penetrating difficult to treat wood species such as Douglas-fir or larch. CCA treatment solution also contains hexavalent chromium, although it rapidly converts to trivalent chromium in the treated wood. Because of the chromium, CCA treating solution and treated wood is less corrosive than many of the other copper-based waterborne preservatives. CCA is classified as a RUP by the EPA.

## Coal-Tar Creosote

Coal-tar creosote is the oldest wood preservative still in commercial use and remains the primary preservative used to protect wood used in railroad construction. It is made by distilling the coal tar that is obtained after high-temperature carbonization of coal. Unlike the other oil-type preservatives, creosote is not usually dissolved in oil, but it does have properties that make it look and feel oily. Creosote contains a chemically complex mixture of organic molecules, most of which are polycyclic aromatic hydrocarbons (PAHs). The composition of creosote depends on the method of distillation and is somewhat variable. However, the small differences in composition within modern creosotes do not significantly affect its performance as a wood preservative. Creosote is standardized at retentions ranging from 128–192 kg/m³ (8–12 lb/ft³) for above ground and ground-contact applications. The efficacy of creosote has been well-established through in-service performance and field tests (Table 2). Creosote-treated posts installed at FPL's test in in southern Mississippi had estimated 54 years to

**Table 2. Estimated years to failure for Southern Pine posts in Mississippi (25 replicates per treatment group)[a]**

| Preservative | Retention (kg/m$^3$) | AWPA retention[b] (%) | Failed (%) | Estimated years to failure | Years to failure 90% confidence limits Lower | Upper |
|---|---|---|---|---|---|---|
| Copper naph (oil) | 0.48 | 44–55 | 46 | 65 | 55 | 78 |
| Coal-tar creosote | 89.60 | 56–70 | 65 | 54 | 47 | 62 |
| Pentachlorophenol | 5.12 | 64–80 | 29 | 74 | 60 | 91 |
| ACA (ACZA) | 5.44 | 68–85 | 52 | 60 | 51 | 69 |
| Untreated | 0 | NA | 100 | 2 | 2 | 3 |

[a]Adapted from Davidson (1977) and Freeman et al. (2006).

[b]These posts were treated to retentions well below current AWPA standards. Values in this column show the tested retention as a percentage of AWPA standard retention for posts (AWPA 2012).

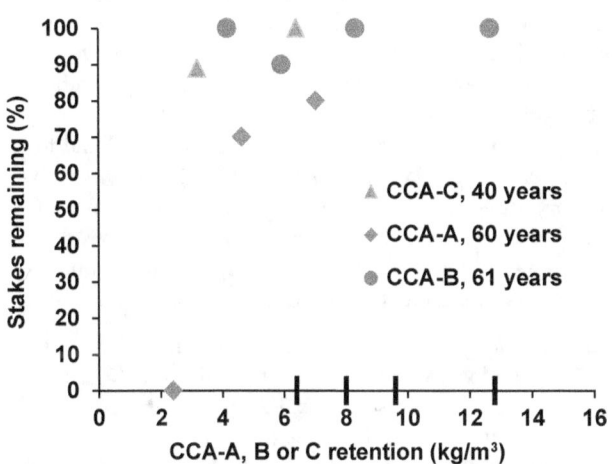

Figure 4. Durability of CCA-treated 2- by 4-in. (nominal) Southern Pine stakes exposed for 40, 60, or 61 years in Mississippi. Solid black lines on x-axis indicate range of AWPA standard retentions for wood to be used in ground contact.

failure despite their relatively low retentions (Freeman et al. 2006). Although an increase in durability is not necessarily directly proportional to an increase in retention, the longevity of these posts would have been expected to be much greater if treated to current AWPA standards. The durability of creosote-treated posts in southern Mississippi is slightly below that reported for posts exposed in South Carolina. In that study, posts treated with creosote retentions ranging from 64 to 128 kg/m$^3$ (4–8 lb/ft$^3$) had approximately 30% failures after 50 years of exposure (Webb et al. 2010). Much greater durability was also reported for creosote-treated posts exposed near Corvallis, Oregon (Morrell et al. 1999) or Ontario, Canada (Morris and Ingram 2010). The greater durability reported for posts exposed in Oregon and Canada may reflect the lower decay hazard in cooler northern climates. The Oregon test location falls into AWPA Hazard Zone 3 (Intermediate), while the more northerly Ontario site is in Hazard Zone 2 (Moderate). In contrast, southern

Mississippi falls into AWPA Hazard Zone 5 (Severe). Wisconsin is in AWPA Hazard Zone 2, suggesting that the durability of creosote-treated posts in Wisconsin would be more similar to that in Oregon or southern Canada.

Creosote-treated wood has a dark-brown to black color and a noticeable odor, which some people consider unpleasant. Workers sometimes object to creosote-treated wood because it soils their clothes and photosensitizes the skin upon contact. The treated wood sometimes also has an oily surface, and patches of creosote sometimes accumulate, creating a skin contact hazard. However, creosote-treated wood has advantages to offset concerns with its appearance and odor. It has lengthy record of satisfactory use in a wide range of applications and a relatively low cost. Creosote is also effective in protecting both hardwoods and softwoods, and is often thought to improve the dimensional stability of the treated wood. With the use of heated solutions and lengthy pressure periods, creosote can be fairly effective at penetrating even fairly difficult to treat wood species. Creosote treatment also does not accelerate, and may even inhibit, the rate of corrosion of metal fasteners relative to untreated wood. Three formulations of creosote are listed in AWPA Standards. CR is straight coal tar distillate, CR-S may be a mixture of coal tar and coal tar distillate, and CR-PS may contain up to 50% petroleum solvent. The retentions in Table 1 are based on straight-run creosote (CR), but in most cases CR-S and CR-PS are standardized at the same retentions. Creosote is a classified as a RUP by the EPA.

### Copper Azole (CA-B and CA-C, ESR-1721, ESR-2240)

Copper azole relies primarily on the preservative properties of copper but also has small amounts of azole fungicides to protect from attack by copper-tolerant fungi. In the "traditional" copper azole formulations, which are standardized by the AWPA, the copper is solubilized in ethanolamine in a manner similar to ACQ Types A, C, and D. CA-B has an actives ratio of 96.1% Cu and 3.9% tebuconazole, while CA-C has an actives ratio of 96.1% Cu, 1.95% tebuconazole, and 1.95% propiconazole. AWPA standardized retentions for copper azole range from 0.96 kg/m$^3$ (0.06 lb/ft$^3$) for

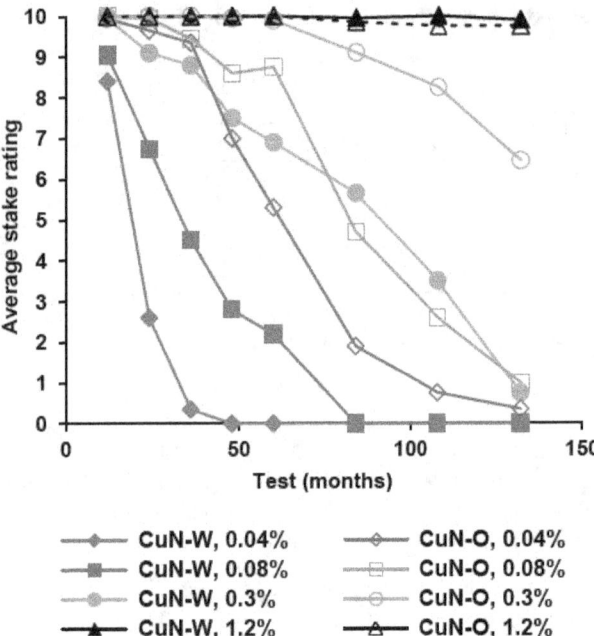

**Figure 5. Durability of 19- by 19-mm (¾- by ¾-in.) Southern Pine stakes treated with water or oilborne copper naphthenate and exposed in southern Mississippi.**

above-ground applications to 6.6 kg/m³ (0.41 lb/ft³) for terrestrial piles. As with other copper-ethanolamine formulations, compatibility with aluminum is a concern. Availability of wood treated with the copper-ethanolamine formulations has also become more limited because many treaters have converted to the analogous "particulate" formulations of copper azole. The "particulate" formulations of copper azole are listed by the International Code Commission under ESR-1721. These formulations, which are some times referred to as µCA-B and µCA-C, have the same copper and azole compositions as the soluble copper formulations. A particulate formulation of CA-B is also listed under ESR-2240. The ESR retentions specified for the particulate formulations tend to be lower than those listed for the ethanolamine formulations in AWPA standards. The particulate copper azole formulations are expected to be less corrosive to aluminum than the ethanolamine formulations. Wood treated with particulate copper azole formulations is widely available.

## Copper Naphthenate (CuN)

Copper naphthenate has been used as a wood preservative since the 1940s, although it is not as widely used as creosote, CCA, or pentachlorophenol. It is an organometallic compound formed as a reaction product of copper salts and petroleum-derived naphthenic acids. In recent years, it has been increasingly used as an alternative to pentachlorophenol. Copper naphthenate has been primarily used as an oil-based formulation, but a water-based formulation (CuN-W) containing ethanolamine has also been standardized by the

AWPA for pressure treatment. The heavy solvent formulation generally provides the greatest durability, and CuN in heavy solvent is currently used for pressure treatment of poles, timbers, and glulam beams. It is standardized by AWPA for retentions ranging from 0.64 kg/m³ (0.04 lb/ft³) for above-ground use to 1.92 kg/m³ (0.12 lb/ft³) for heavy duty ground-contact applications (retentions expressed as elemental copper). Although copper naphthenate does not have as extensive a history of in-service durability as CCA, creosote, or pentachlorophenol, its efficacy has been demonstrated in field tests. Copper naphthenate posts exposed in southern Mississippi had expected service lives of 65 years despite being treated to only about half the current AWPA retention for posts (Freeman et al. 2006) (Table 2). The durability of copper-naphthenate treated posts in the Mississippi study is slightly less than that reported by Morris and Ingram (2010), who noted only one failure after 58 years for posts exposed near Ontario, Canada. Copper naphthenate is also dissolved in light solvent for pressure treatment of above-ground members (such as glulam beams) and for brush-on application to untreated wood exposed when cutting pressure-treated wood. Most commercial pressure-treating facilities are using copper naphthenate in heavy solvent. It is also used for non-pressure steeping (extended dipping) treatment of round fence posts in some western states.

The CuN-W standardized retentions range from 1.1 kg/m³ (0.07 lb/ft³) for above-ground use to 1.76 kg/m³ (0.11 lb/ft³) for ground-contact applications. FPL researchers compared the durability of stakes treated with oil and waterborne formulations of copper naphthenate and found that the oilborne formulations were more durable at lower concentrations (Fig. 5). However, at the highest concentration evaluated (1.2% copper) both formulations were highly effective. Waterborne copper naphthenate does contain soluble copper ions and might be expected to contribute somewhat to corrosion of aluminum. Waterborne copper naphthenate has less obvious odor than the oil-borne formulation, but the odor is noticeable until the wood dries. There are no or limited pressure-treatment facilities currently using CUN-W.

## KDS

KDS is another pressure-treatment preservative formulation that uses copper solubilized with ethanolamine along with a co-biocide (in this case polymeric betaine). It is produced in two formulations: the KDS formulation also contains boron, and has an actives composition of 47% copper oxide, 23% polymeric betaine, and 30% boric acid. KDS–B does not contain boron (nomenclature is non-intuitive here) and has an actives composition of 68% copper oxide and 32% polymeric betaine. KDS is standardized by AWPA for treatment of commodities used above ground and for general use in contact with soil at retentions ranging from 3.04–7.52 kg/m³ (0.19–0.47 lb/ft³). AWPA standards do not list KDS or KDS-B for severe exposures or critical applications, but they are listed for these uses under ICC-ESR 2500. The soluble copper used in KDS might be expected to increase the risk of corrosion of aluminum. Although availability of KDS is somewhat limited, a few treating plants are in the United States using this preservative.

## Pentachlorophenol

Pentachlorophenol has been widely used as a pressure treatment since the 1940s. The active ingredients, chlorinated phenols, are crystalline solids that can be dissolved in different types of organic solvents. The performance of pentachlorophenol and the properties of the treated wood are influenced by the properties of the solvent. The heavy oil solvent is generally used when the treated wood is to be used in ground contact because wood treated with lighter solvents is slightly less durable in such exposures. Wood treated with pentachlorophenol in heavy oil typically has a brown color and may have a slightly oily surface that is difficult to paint. It also has some odor, which is associated with the solvent. Like creosote, it is effective in protecting both hardwoods and softwoods and is often thought to improve the dimensional stability of the treated wood. Pentachlorophenol in heavy oil has long been a popular choice for treatment of utility poles, bridge timbers, glulam beams, and foundation piling. The treated wood is quite durable, as shown in Table 2 (Freeman et al. 2006) and Figure 6. Lighter solvents are often used for treatment of wood in above-ground applications, but pentachlorophenol-light solvent treatments also provide substantial durability at higher retentions (Fig. 6). Lighter solvents provide the advantage of a less oily surface, lighter color, and less odor. However, one disadvantage of the lighter oil is that less water repellency is imparted to the wood. With the use of heated solutions and extended pressure periods, pentachlorophenol is fairly effective at penetrating difficult to treat species. Pentachlorophenol treatment does not accelerate corrosion relative to untreated wood. Pentachlorophenol is classified as a RUP by the EPA.

# Corrosion Aspects of Selecting Preservatives for Sign Posts

## Mechanism of Corrosion in Treated Wood

Corrosion is a redox reaction, where a metal is oxidized (loses electrons) and another species in the solution or atmosphere is reduced (gains electrons). Corrosion is nearly always thermodynamically favorable; what is more important is the kinetics of the reaction. Put more simply, corrosion will always happen, but it can be slowed to where it is not important.

Zelinka and Stone (2011) have demonstrated that the corrosion mechanism in treated wood involves the reduction of free cupric ions in the wood preservative. The mechanism is illustrated in Figure 7. Importantly, this mechanism is based upon (1) copper-based wood preservatives and (2) the metal fastener being anodic to copper on the galvanic series. Most construction metals are anodic to copper and will

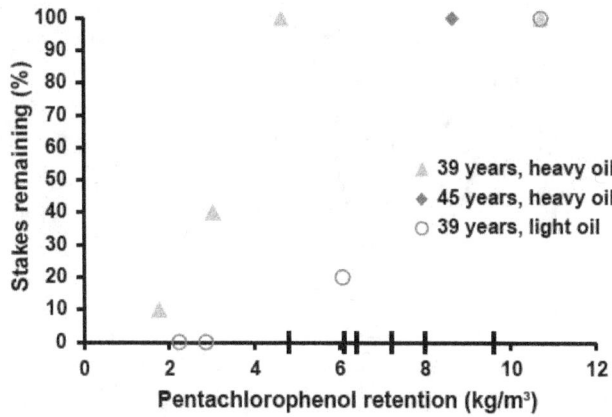

Figure 6. Durability of 2- by 4-in. (nominal) Southern Pine stakes treated with pentachlorophenol and exposed in Mississippi. Solid black lines on x-axis indicate range of AWPA standard retentions for wood to be used in ground contact.

corrode; the notable exception is stainless steel. The corrosion mechanism involves diffusion of the cupric ions to the metal surface, where they are reduced as the metal is oxidized. This mechanism is thermodynamically favorable and will occur. What is important is the rate-limiting step that controls the kinetics and thus how rapidly the metal will corrode. In theory, the rate-limiting step could be the diffusion of ions to the metal surface or the oxidation/reduction reaction at the metal surface. Several different experiments have demonstrated that the rate-limiting step is not diffusion but rather the reaction at the metal surface (Baker 1992; Zelinka and Rammer 2009; Zelinka and Stone 2011). This has large implications for corrosion as it implies that the corrosion rate will not decrease with time as it does in atmospheric corrosion (Zelinka et al. 2011).

It is important to emphasize that the corrosion of metals in contact with treated wood is much different than atmospheric corrosion. Although the wood may be exposed to the atmosphere, corrosion of embedded fasteners is controlled by wood chemistry and moisture. This difference in environment has two important implications: (1) zinc-galvanization is ineffective, and (2) the corrosion rate does not decrease with time. Since these points seem counterintuitive, they will be expanded upon in the next two paragraphs.

In atmospheric corrosion, zinc oxidizes to form hydrozincite ($Zn_5(CO_3)_2(OH)_6$) and smithsonite ($ZnCO_3$), which passivate the zinc surface; that is, these oxidized species protect the metal from further corrosion. Conversely, steel forms goethite ($\alpha$-FeOOH), also called "red-rust" in atmospheric conditions.

Kinetically, hydrozincite and smithsonite are better at protecting the underlying metal than goethite; that is why zinc corrodes more slowly than steel in atmospheric conditions (Zhang 2003). It is known that in certain environments, such

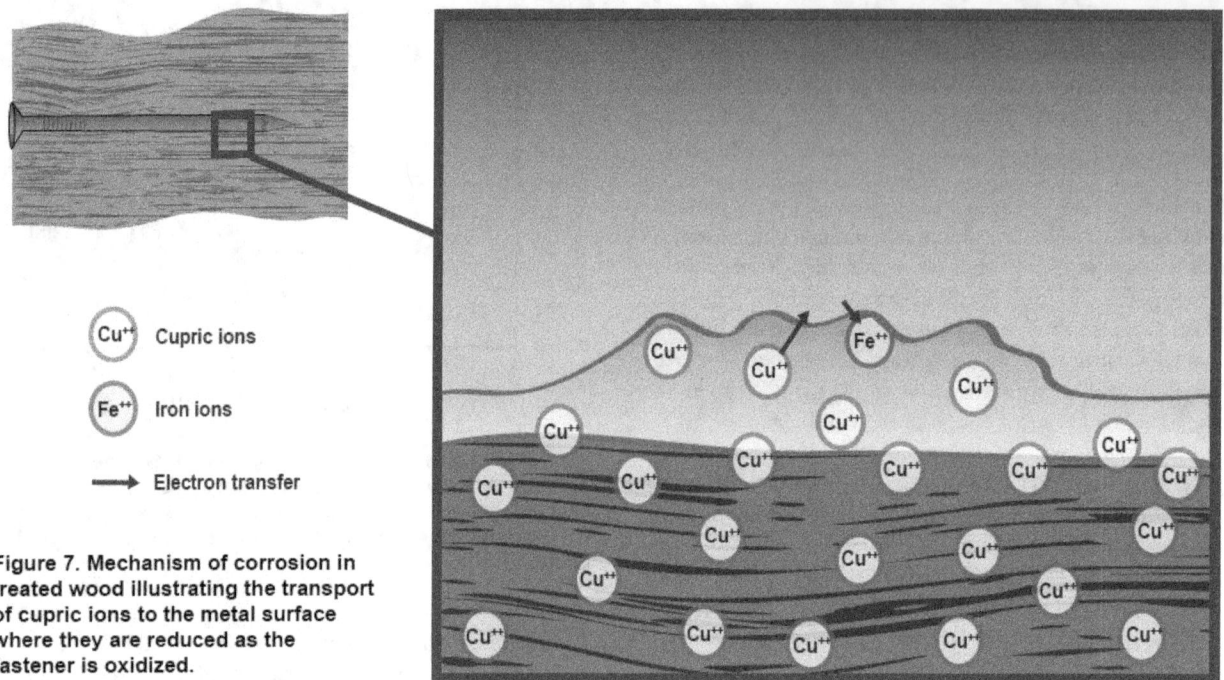

Cu⁺⁺ Cupric ions

Fe⁺⁺ Iron ions

→ Electron transfer

**Figure 7. Mechanism of corrosion in treated wood illustrating the transport of cupric ions to the metal surface where they are reduced as the fastener is oxidized.**

as immersion in saltwater (Zhang et al. 1998) or in environments with volatile acetic and formic acids (Knotkova-Cermakova and Vlckova 1971), different corrosion products form and zinc corrodes more rapidly than steel. In addition to measuring the corrosion rates, Zelinka et al. (2010) examined the corrosion products on fasteners removed from steel and galvanized steel fasteners in wood using X-ray diffraction and did not observe smithsonite on the zinc fasteners. Instead, they observed hydrozincite, namuwite ($Zn_2(SO_4)$ $(OH)_6 \cdot 4H_2O$), and simonkolleite ($Zn_5(OH)_8Cl_2 \cdot (H2O)$), which are consistent with the observed relative corrosion rates.

During atmospheric corrosion, in many cases the corrosion rate decreases with time because of passivation. Empirically, the kinetics are frequently described by

$$\Delta W = Kt^n \qquad (1)$$

where $\Delta W$ is the change in weight, $K$ is a constant (the 1-year corrosion rate), $t$ is the time in years, and $n$ is an exponent that controls the kinetics and describes passivation (Legault and Preban 1975). Theoretically, $n$ should be bounded by 0.5, which represents complete diffusion control, and 1, which represents "activation control," where the rate-determining step is the electron transfer reaction at the metal surface. In wood, $n = 1$ behavior has been observed by several researchers, which unfortunately represents a worst case scenario (Baker 1992; Zelinka and Rammer 2009; Zelinka and Stone 2011).

## Review of Corrosion Data from New Wood Preservatives

Since the 2004 change in wood preservative regulation, there have been several investigations of the corrosiveness of metals in contact with treated wood. The studies cover a wide range of preservatives, preservative retentions, wood moisture contents, and metals tested. Not surprisingly, a wide variation in corrosion rates have been reported (e.g., from 2–113 µm/y for galvanized steel in ACQ-treated wood). Because of the wide variations of test conditions used, it is best to only compare results within a single study or across different studies with very similar conditions.

Many of the design recommendations for materials selection in wood are based off of the recommendations of Baker (1992), who conducted a 17-year investigation of corrosion of metal fasteners embedded into chromated copper arsenate- (CCA-) and ammoniacal copper arsenate- (ACA-) treated wood and exposed either underground or in a room maintained near 100% RH. From these data, Baker concluded that at a minimum, hot-dip galvanized fasteners should be used in treated wood and cautioned against the use of aluminum fasteners. Importantly, Baker presented the corrosion data as a percentage of weight loss instead of a true corrosion rate because he could not calculate the surface area of threaded fasteners. Zelinka and Rammer reanalyzed Baker's data using data in Baker's laboratory notebook and an algorithm they had developed to measure the surface area of threaded fasteners (Baker 1992; Rammer and Zelinka 2008; Rammer and Zelinka 2010). They found that when the corrosion rate was adjusted to a true corrosion rate, the corrosion rate of aluminum was in fact less than hot-dip galvanized steel. Baker (1992) also reported that pitting was observed on the aluminum fasteners. However, Zelinka and Rammer could not determine any evidence of pitting corrosion in similar exposure tests conducted for one year, nor could they find any evidence of pitting corrosion in photographs in Baker's laboratory notebook.

Zelinka has published results of several different corrosion tests that were conducted at 27 °C (80 °F) and 100% RH (Zelinka 2007; Zelinka and Rammer 2009; Zelinka et al. 2010; Zelinka and Stone 2011). In one study, Zelinka and Rammer (2009) examined the corrosion of five different metal fasteners (carbon steel, hot-dip galvanized steel, electroplated galvanized steel, aluminum, and stainless steel) embedded in wood treated with ACQ to a retention of 4 kg/m$^{-3}$. They found that the corrosion rate of hot-dip galvanized steel (in µm/y) was the highest (62) followed by carbon steel (34), aluminum (22), and electroplated galvanized steel (21). The corrosion rate of stainless steel was statistically indistinguishable from zero. In another study (Zelinka et al. 2010), steel and hot-dip galvanized steel fasteners were exposed to six different wood treatments: chromated copper arsenate (CCA), alkaline copper quaternary (ACQ-D), copper azole (CuAz-B), micronized copper quaternary (MCQ), didecyldimethylammonium carbonate (DDAC, or the "quat" in ACQ and MCQ). For galvanized steel, ACQ was the most corrosive (32 µm/y), followed by CuAz (29), MCQ (19), CCA (16), DDAC (5.5), and untreated (4.4). For carbon steel, the order was slightly different: ACQ (17), MCQ (13), CuAz (11), CCA (10), DDAC (1.9), and untreated (0.7).

Kear et al. (2009) examined the corrosion of three different metals (316 stainless steel, hot-dip galvanized steel, and plain carbon steel) in three different preservatives (CCA, ACQ, CuAz), treated to three different retention levels with four different test methodologies. The retention levels were specified in a New Zealand standard that specifies a mass basis (i.e., kg/kg) instead of a density basis and therefore cannot be directly compared with traditional U.S. retentions (in lb/ft$^3$ or kg/m$^3$). Differences in the corrosiveness of the preservatives were most apparent in a constant exposure to 90% relative humidity (RH). Corrosion rates were (CCA:CuAz:ACQ) 4:14:45 µm/y$^{-1}$ for mild steel fasteners and 5:16:26 µm/y for hot-dip galvanized steel fasteners. Average corrosion rates as high as 113 µm/y were observed for galvanized steel in ACQ treated wood in a "moisture saturated air" condition.

Simpson Strong Tie Corporation (Pleasanton, CA) published a technical bulletin on the results of in-house AWPA-E12 (AWPA 2007) corrosion tests they had conducted (Simpson Strong-Tie 2008). In this test method, a metal plate is sandwiched between two blocks of wood and exposed to a high temperature (50 °C), high humidity (90% RH) environment. They found that the corrosiveness of ACQ-D (carbonate) was roughly equivalent to that of CuAz, and both of these were more than twice as corrosive as CCA-C. They also found that ACZA was more than three times more corrosive than CCA and that borates were less corrosive than CCA. A footnote in the table mentioned that for micronized formulations like MCQ the "relative corrosiveness is somewhat lower than ACQ-D."

Copper naphthenate is sometimes used as a preservative in timber bridges. While there are no peer-reviewed data on the corrosiveness of copper naphthenate, Anthony Forest Products Company (El Dorado, AK) published a technical bulletin with the results of AWPA E12 tests that compares both the waterborne and oilborne formulations of copper naphthenate against ACQ-D and CCA-C for mild steel, hot-dip galvanized steel, aluminum, and red brass (Anthony Forest Products Company 2013). Although no data are given on the variability between replicates, the data clearly suggest that either formulation of copper naphthenate is much less corrosive than ACQ and possibly less corrosive than CCA. For mild steel, the corrosion rates (in mils (0.001 in.) per year) were 4.9 for ACQ, 1.0 for CCA, 0.17 for waterborne copper naphthenate, and 0.03 for the oilborne formulation. An even larger difference was observed for aluminum, where the corrosion rates were 7.3 for ACQ, 0.3 for CCA, 0.07 for waterborne copper naphthenate, and 0 for the oilborne formulation. Although this bulletin was published by a company that supplies products treated with copper napthenate, the data suggest that copper naphthenate is much less corrosive than ACQ and less than or equal in corrosiveness to CCA.

Freeman and McIntyre (2008) summarized the results of several unpublished corrosion tests of pressure-treated wood in contact with different metals which compared traditional (ACQ and CuAz) against their micronized formulations (MCQ and mCuAz). Most of the data shown was from AWPA E-12 tests. The results are inconclusive. In one test, the micronized formulation of CuAz is less corrosive than the standard formulation for galvanized steel but more corrosive for plain carbon steel and the micronized formulation is much more corrosive to aluminum. The remainder of the E-12 data have similar trends; in some cases the micronized formulations show lower corrosiveness; in other cases, the traditional formulations appear less corrosive. The only results that consistently show that the micronized formulations are less corrosive than the traditional formulations are from a test conducted using a protocol from the International Staple and Nail Tool Association (ISANTA, La Grange, IL). In this test, the micronized formulations appear slightly (approximately 30%–40%) less corrosive, with the notable exception of aluminum, in which case the micronized formulations are more corrosive.

## Special Corrosion Considerations for Sign Posts

The purpose of this literature review is to develop recommendations to minimize corrosion in signs attached to treated wood posts. WisDOT noticed severe corrosion of aluminum signs attached to posts treated with alkaline copper quaternary (ACQ), which is detailed in Final Report WI-06-04 (Wilson 2004). WisDOT currently attaches aluminum signs to CCA-treated posts with galvanized lag screws. Excessive corrosion was noted around the bolt hole; this suggests that a galvanic couple was occurring between the lag screw and the sign post that accelerated the corrosion of the aluminum sign post. Since the failure of the sign appears to be caused by galvanic corrosion, it is worthwhile to have a brief discussion of galvanic corrosion and discuss prevention strategies.

Galvanic corrosion happens when three conditions are satisfied: (1) two dissimilar metals (2) are placed in electrical contact (3) in the presence of an electrolyte. If any of the three conditions are not met (i.e., metals are not in electrical contact, metals are not in an electrolyte), galvanic corrosion cannot occur. In the case of the sign posts, the electrolyte is the wood, and the metals are in electrical contact because the galvanized bolt head is in contact with the aluminum sign post. When the conditions for galvanic corrosion are met, the more active metal (called the anode) will corrode more rapidly than it would otherwise corrode and the more noble metal (called the cathode) will corrode more slowly than it would otherwise corrode. Whether a metal is active or noble to another metal depends upon the thermodynamics of the oxidation reactions in that environment.

It is important to point out a couple of common misunderstandings of galvanic corrosion at this point. For instance, commonly it is assumed that only the anode ("sacrificial anode") corrodes in a galvanic couple. This is not true; both metals corrode, but the cathode may corrode slowly enough that it does not fail in a normal service life. The second common misperception is that there is a single "galvanic series" that one can use to tell if a given metal will be active in a given environment. While galvanic series have been tabulated for seawater and other electrolytes (Matsukawa et al. 2011), the positions of metals can change dramatically depending on the environment.

From the WisDOT final report (Wilson 2004), it is clear that galvanic corrosion is occurring and that in ACQ-treated wood, zinc is cathodic (more noble) to aluminum, and the aluminum signs failed because of galvanic corrosion near the fastener. If the galvanic corrosion could be stopped, it is possible that the signs would last much longer. As it is not possible to change the metals used or the electrolyte, the only way to prevent galvanic corrosion in this situation is to electrically isolate the bolt from the aluminum sign. This should be possible by using a nonconductive washer

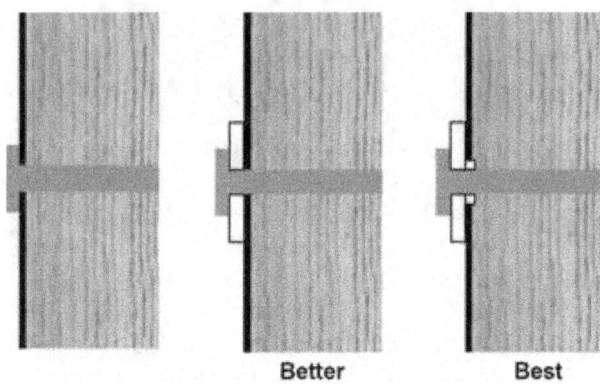

**Better**   **Best**

**Figure 8. Strategies to mitigate galvanic corrosion. A non-conductive washer between the head of the lag screw and the sign should eliminate electrical contact between the bolt and the sign (Better). If there is a tight clearance between the hole and the bolt, it might be necessary to coat the edge of the holes to prevent electrical contact (Best).**

between the head of the lag screw and the wooden post (Fig. 8).

### Corrosion Recommendations

- The corrosion of metals in contact with wood is different from atmospheric corrosion.

- The corrosion is extremely sensitive to the wood moisture content. Preventing the wood from getting wet, if possible, is the easiest way to prevent corrosion.

- Existing corrosion data are somewhat dependent on how the tests were conducted. Despite this, it appears that the relative corrosiveness of different preservatives appears to be as follows:

  oil CuN $\leq$ water CuN $\ll$ CCA $<$ MCQ, mCuAz $\approx$ ACQ, CuAz $\ll$ ACZA

- There appears to be a galvanic couple between the zinc galvanized lag screw and the aluminum sign when they are in contact with treated wood. The zinc and aluminum should be separated by a dielectric to increase the service life.

## Summary of Preservatives' Potential for Sign Post Treatments

In this section, the properties of the preservatives are summarized, and they are given a relative ranking regarding the suitability for sign posts. Only those preservatives judged to be effective in protecting wood used in ground contact are discussed. This review indicates that CCA, the preservative currently being used for sign post treatment, remains one of the best options. Another strong candidate is oil-based copper naphthenate, but the possibility of worker concerns associated with the odor and the potentially oily surface may need to be assessed.

## Water-Based Preservatives

Water-based preservatives have the general advantage of leaving posts with relatively low odor and clean surface. As a group, they also tend to not be as effective in protecting hardwood species as the oil-based preservatives, although this limitation can be overcome through the use of higher retentions. Water-based preservatives may increase the likelihood of signpost warping as the wood dries after treatment.

### CCA

CCA, the preservative currently used by the Wisconsin DOT and by other states, remains a strong candidate for treatment of sign posts. It has decades of proven efficacy, is readily available, and is compatible with aluminum. On the negative side, CCA does not penetrate refractory wood species as well as some of the other preservatives (such as ACZA and ACQ-B) that use ammonia and can be heated during treatment. CCA is also a RUP that contains arsenic. However, CCA was recently re-registered by the EPA, and current regulatory concerns appear to be focused on improving worker safety at pressure-treatment facilities.

- Suitability for use with current pine species: High
- Suitability for use with less treatable softwoods: Medium-high
- Suitability for use with hardwoods: Medium
- Overall potential: High

### Particulate Copper Preservatives (Micronized Copper Quat, Micronized Copper Azole)

These formulations have become widely available and have been used to some extent by Wisconsin DOT for treatment of sign posts. They have not been in use long enough to document their ability to provide long-term durability, but short-term stake testing indicates that potential. These formulations do not contain arsenic, chromium, or other RUPs, and thus may be less likely to be restricted by regulatory agencies. The use of the particulate rather than soluble copper decreases, but does not eliminate, concerns about corrosiveness toward aluminum, and additional steps may be needed to minimize corrosion. These formulations may have difficulty penetrating refractory wood species and there are little data on their ability to protect hardwoods.

- Suitability for use with current pine species: Medium-high (corrosion concerns)
- Suitability for use with less treatable softwoods: Low (penetration problems)
- Suitability for use with hardwoods: Medium (little data, but probably similar to other water-based preservatives)
- Overall potential: Medium-high

### Water-Based Copper Naphthenate

Water-based copper naphthenate has seen little commercial pressure-treatment use, but stake testing indicates that it is an effective preservative. There is relatively little information on its ability to penetrate refractory wood species. Water-based copper naphthenate solution is available for consumer purchase and application, and thus restriction from use as a pressure-treatment preservative does not appear likely. The compatibility of water-based copper naphthenate with aluminum has not been well documented, but corrosion is expected to be relatively low. A major disadvantage of water-based copper naphthenate is its lack of availability as a pressure-treatment preservative.

- Suitability for use with current pine species: Medium (availability)
- Suitability for use with less treatable softwoods: Medium (availability)
- Suitability for use with hardwoods: Medium-low (efficacy, availability)
- Overall potential: Medium

### ACZA

ACZA is an effective preservative with a long history of commercial use. Because of the ammonia used in the formulation, it is better able to penetrate refractory wood species than some other water-based preservatives and has been widely used for treatment of Douglas-fir. It has also been standardized by AWPA for treatment of hardwood railroad ties. However, like CCA it contains arsenic and is a RUP. It is less available than CCA, although it is being used by a treatment facility in Minnesota. A potential disadvantage of this preservative is corrosiveness to aluminum. Although several states do include ACZA in their sign post specifications, manufacturers do not recommend that aluminum be placed in direct contact with ACZA-treated wood. It is possible that states with ACZA in their sign-post specifications are either not actually using it or are using it with signs made with other materials.

- Suitability for use with current pine species: Medium-low (corrosion concerns)
- Suitability for use with less treatable softwoods: Medium-low (corrosion concerns)
- Suitability for use with hardwoods: Medium-low (corrosion concerns)
- Overall potential: Medium

### Soluble Copper Preservatives (ACQ, Copper Azole, KDS, Copper-HDO)

ACQ has been used commercially for nearly two decades and has established an accompanying level of confidence in its ability to protect wood from decay. Copper azole has a slightly shorter history of use, but it and the other copper-based systems are likely to provide adequate protection at equivalent copper concentrations. These formulations do not contain arsenic and chromium, and may be less likely to face regulatory scrutiny than those preservatives classified as restricted-use pesticides. They are also relatively capable of penetrating a range of wood species, especially if ammonia is used in the formulation. Some of these preservatives (particularly ACQ) are commercially available. However, these preservatives can be damaging to aluminum signs, as demonstrated by prior WisDOT observations (Wilson 2004).

- Suitability for use with current pine species: Medium-low (corrosion concerns)

- Suitability for use with less treatable softwoods: Medium-low (corrosion concerns)

- Suitability for use with hardwoods: Medium-low (efficacy, corrosion concerns)

- Overall potential: Medium

## Acid Copper Chromate (ACC)

ACC has been a commercial wood preservative for decades, although not used as widely as other wood preservatives. Although wood treated with ACC is generally durable, studies indicate that it is vulnerable to the copper-tolerant fungi that occur in some locations. The practical impact of this vulnerability is unclear because the distribution and prevalence of these types of fungi is unknown. Although ACC does not contain arsenic, the treatment solution does contain hexavalent chromium, and the EPA has restricted its use to applications similar to CCA. Like CCA, ACC is expected to cause little corrosion of aluminum. A major limitation of ACC is its lack of availability.

- Suitability for use with current pine species: Medium-low (availability, efficacy)

- Suitability for use with less treatable softwoods: Medium-low (availability, efficacy)

- Suitability for use with hardwoods: Low (availability, efficacy)

- Overall potential: Medium

## Oil-Based Preservatives

Oil-based preservatives are less likely to cause warping of sign posts, and tend to be more compatible with hardwoods than the water-based preservatives. Their major disadvantages are odor and the potential for having an oily surface.

## Copper Naphthenate (Oil-Based)

Although not as widely used as preservatives such as creosote, pentachlorophenol and CCA, oil-based copper naphthenate has a long history of commercial use (Fig. 9) and its efficacy has been demonstrated in long-term post

Figure 9. Oil-based copper naphthenate is sometimes used for treatment of salt storage sheds.

tests. Although not as widely available as some other preservatives, there are to be pressure-treatment facilities in Michigan and South Dakota using oil-based copper naphthenate. Copper naphthenate solution is available for consumer application, and is unlikely to be restricted from pressure-treatment application. It is also compatible with aluminum. The primary disadvantages of copper naphthenate are its odor and the possibility of the treated wood having an oily surface.

- Suitability for use with current pine species: High

- Suitability for use with less treatable softwoods: Medium-high (lack of data on treatability)

- Suitability for use with hardwoods: High

- Overall potential: Medium-high (overall rating reduced because of the potential for worker concerns with odor and oily surface)

## Pentachlorophenol

Pentachlorophenol has a long history of use and proven efficacy as a wood preservative. Although not as widely available as some other preservatives, there are pressure-treatment facilities in Minnesota, Missouri, and Iowa using pentachlorophenol. Pentachlorophenol is classified as a RUP by EPA and has the associated safety and handling concerns. It is compatible with aluminum, but the treated wood has an odor and the potential for an oily surface.

- Suitability for use with current pine species: Medium-high (possible worker concerns)

- Suitability for use with less treatable softwoods: Medium-high (possible worker concerns)

- Suitability for use with hardwoods: Medium-high (possible worker concerns)

- Overall potential: Medium-high

## Creosote

Creosote has a long history of use and is an effective preservative. It has been used more widely and with a broader range of wood species than any other preservative. There are currently fewer treating plants using creosote than other types of preservatives, but there is a facility producing creosote-treated wood in Wisconsin. Like the other oil-based preservatives, creosote is compatible with aluminum. Creosote is a restricted-use pesticide and has a strong odor. It is also a skin sensitizer and may elicit concerns from workers handling the treated wood.

- Suitability for use with current pine species: Medium (possible worker concerns)

- Suitability for use with less treatable softwoods: Medium (possible worker concerns)

- Suitability for use with hardwoods: Medium (possible worker concerns)

- Overall potential: Medium-high

# Wood Species Options for Wisconsin DOT Signposts

## Wood Species Currently Listed in WisDOT Signpost Specifications

Sign posts are specified in "Section 634, Wood and Tubular Steel Sign Posts." That specification refers to "Section 614.2.5, Wood Posts and Offset Blocks," for a listing of wood species. The species listed are Southern Pine, red pine, ponderosa pine, jack pine, white pine, Hem-Fir, oak, Douglas-fir, western hemlock, and western larch. In this section we discuss the characteristics of these wood species (or species groups) as they relate to use for Wisconsin sign posts.

## Southern Pine

Southern Pine is currently used by the Wisconsin DOT for sign posts. Southern Pine is a grouping of wood species grown in the southeastern United States and includes loblolly (*Pinus taeda*), longleaf (*P. paulstris*), shortleaf (*P. echinata*), and slash pine (*P. elliottii*). Southern Pine wood species are commonly used for preservative treatment because they are relatively strong (among softwoods) and have a large, easily treated sapwood zone. Southern Pine is the most readily available treated wood species east of the Rocky Mountains and is a reasonable choice for use in Wisconsin sign posts. It is also worth noting that the bulk of wood preservative standards and associated research is based on treatment of Southern Pine species. Thus, the treatability of Southern Pine and its durability when adequately treated are better understood than for other wood species. However, Southern Pine does have moderately high shrinkage that can lead to problems with warping, especially in longer sign posts. It is also somewhat of a changing resource, with trees now grown more rapidly than in the past. These faster growing trees have wider growth rings and may have a greater proportion of juvenile wood, which further contributes to warping. In many structures, this warping in treated Southern Pine can be minimized by securely fastening (i.e., screwing or bolting) the members in place before the wood dries. However, this is a less viable option for sign posts.

## Red Pine

Red pine (*P. resinosa*) is a Wisconsin wood species that is currently used by for sign posts by WisDOT. Although red pine is a minor species from a national perspective, it is an important component of the forest resource in Wisconsin (Table 3), Minnesota, Michigan, and northeastern states. It has been widely planted in plantations, which allows for relatively economical harvesting (Fig. 10). Red pine is considered a "treatable" wood species and is often grouped with Southern Pine and ponderosa pine in treatment standards. However, it does appear to be somewhat less easily treated than Southern Pine, or at least less consistently treatable. Gjovik and Schumann (1992) evaluated the treatability of several northeastern wood species and noted that preservative penetration in red pine was generally less than that in eastern white pine (Fig. 11). Variability in the treatability of red pine appears to be associated with geographic source and with the sapwood to heartwood transitional growth rings that visually appear to be sapwood but have permeability more similar to heartwood (Lebow et al. 2006). However, that study also noted that more consistent penetration could be achieved by modifying the treatment conditions. When treated with ground-contact preservatives, red pine is highly durable. Red pine posts thermally treated (a non-pressure process) with creosote to have had no failures after 71 years of exposure at a test site in Ontario, Canada (Morris and Ingram 2010). Posts pressure-treated with pentachlorophenol in heavy solvent have had no failures after 41 years at that test site, which is at approximately the same latitude as Hayward, Wisconsin. Red pine has lower strength properties than Southern Pine species, but higher strength than other pine species such as eastern white and ponderosa pine. Like Southern Pine species, red pine has moderately high shrinkage, which can lead to warping, especially in longer sign posts.

## Ponderosa Pine

Ponderosa pine (*P. ponderosa*) is not a Wisconsin species, but is a major wood species in western states and as far east as the Black Hills of South Dakota. Ponderosa pine is considered a treatable species and is typically grouped with Southern Pine and red pine in treatment standards. However, ponderosa pine is softer and weaker than Southern Pine or red pine, and its use as a treated structural product has been somewhat less common. Ponderosa pine also has a more uniform grain and less shrinkage than southern or red pines, which creates profitable markets in other applications. There is relatively little data on the long-term durability of treated

Table 3. Growth volume and extent of current utilization of major Wisconsin wood species[a]

| Wood species or species grouping[a] | Existing volume ($\times 10^6$ ft³) | Annual growth ($\times 10^6$ ft³) | Annual removals ($\times 10^6$ ft³) | "Unused" growth ($\times 10^6$ ft³)[b] |
|---|---|---|---|---|
| Eastern white pine | 1,667 | 68.7 | 9.4 | 59.3 |
| Soft maple (red, silver) | 2,494 | 75.0 | 31.6 | 43.4 |
| Red pine | 1,646 | 71.4 | 34.5 | 36.9 |
| Hard maple (sugar, black) | 2,367 | 61.2 | 26.5 | 34.7 |
| Ash (white, black, green) | 1,386 | 42.0 | 10.8 | 31.2 |
| Red oaks (red, black, pin) | 2,680 | 58.4 | 39.6 | 18.8 |
| Basswood | 1,204 | 26.9 | 10.7 | 16.2 |
| White oaks (white, burr, swamp) | 1,042 | 17.6 | 10.0 | 7.6 |
| Spruce (white, black) | 460 | 11.2 | 4.5 | 6.7 |
| Eastern hemlock | 459 | 8.0 | 1.7 | 6.3 |
| Elm (American, slippery, rock) | 339 | 3.3 | 1.0 | 2.3 |
| Balsam fir | 410 | 7.0 | 6.1 | 0.9 |
| Yellow birch | 263 | 3.0 | 2.6 | 0.4 |
| Jack pine | 246 | 6.0 | 12.7 | −6.7 |
| Aspen (quaking, bigtooth) | 2,324 | 60.5 | 71.0 | −10.5 |
| Paper birch | 540 | −6.8 | 12.6 | −19.4 |

[a]Adapted from Forest Resources Annual Report (Wisconsin DNR 2012).
http://dnr.wi.gov/topic/ForestBusinesses/documents/WisconsinForestResources.pdf
[b]Annual growth − Annual removals. For relative ranking purposes only. This column was not included in the Wisconsin DNR report.

Figure 10. Red pine has been widely planted in Wisconsin, Minnesota, and Michigan.

ponderosa pine, although one study did report no failures after 30 years for posts pressure-treated with pentachlorophenol in heavy oil and exposed in South Dakota (Markstrom and Gjovik 1992). An earlier report also noted no failures after 27 years for ponderosa pine posts treated with a creosote–oil solution and exposed in South Dakota (Kulp 1966).

## Jack Pine

Jack pine (*P. banksiana*) is a native Wisconsin wood species, but is not currently used for sign posts. The volume of jack pine in Wisconsin is only about one-fifth that of red pine or eastern white pine, and it has suffered declines in growth volume over the last several decades. The diameter of jack pine stems is also typically smaller than that of red pine, eastern white pine, or Southern Pine, somewhat limiting their value in lumber production. In addition, jack pine stems tend to have a greater proportion of less treatable heartwood than do the pine species more commonly used for preservative treatment. When sawn to produce posts, (such as sign posts) there is a higher likelihood that jack pine will have at least two faces with little sapwood remaining. Jack pine is listed as a post species in AWPA standards, but has lesser penetration requirements than red, white, or Southern Pine because of its narrower sapwood band. AWPA standards also specify that sawn jack pine posts be incised (run through rollers that cut many small slits in the wood) prior to treatment to improve the depth and uniformity of preservative penetration (Fig. 12). Incising is not required for round posts on the assumption that they will have an intact outer band of treatable sapwood.

The long-term durability of preservative-treated jack pine posts has not been the subject of extensive research. FPL researchers did expose posts pressure-treated with 5% tetrachlorophenol (precursor to pentachlorophenol) near Madison, Wisconsin, and reported no failures after 29 years. Jack pine is an important component of the Canadian species mix, and several post durability tests have been conducted at a test site in Ontario, Canada. Only 1 of 20 jack pine posts treated with creosote by a thermal (non-pressure process) have failed after 71 years of exposure and only 1 of 14 posts pressure treated with copper naphthenate have failed after 58 years (Morris and Ingram 2010). Posts pressure treated

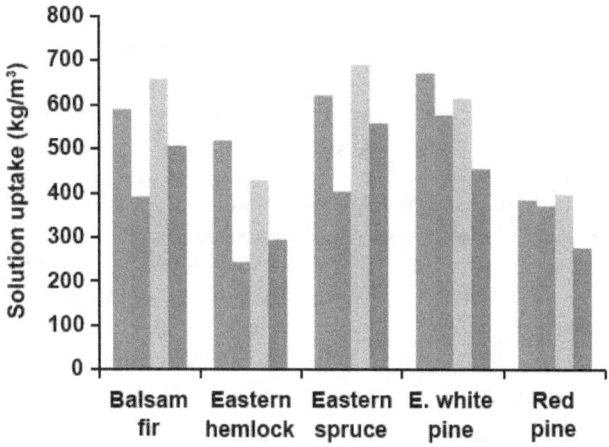

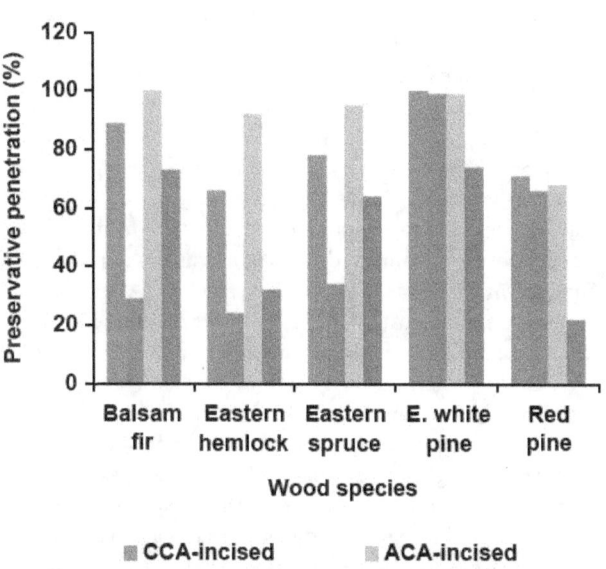

Figure 12. Incising is used on less treatable wood species to improve depth and uniformity of treatment.

**CCA-incised**    **ACA-incised**

**CCA-unincised**    **ACA-unincised**

Figure 11. Preservative uptake and penetration for CCA- or ACA-treated incised or unincised northeastern softwoods. Note: Eastern white and red pine specimens were predominately composed of less treatable heartwood. Adapted from Gjovik and Schumann (1992).

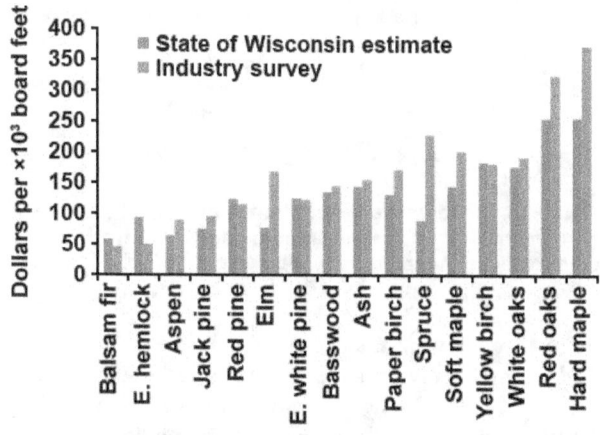

Figure 13. Stumpage value of saw timber as estimated by the State of Wisconsin or an industry survey. Source: Adapted from Wisconsin DNR (2012). The State of Wisconsin estimate is based on the total value of timber sales and products produced; the industry survey is a survey of prices reported by timber buyers, sellers, and their agents.

with CCA formulations have also been very durable, with no failures after 57 years for posts treated to 5.1 kg/m³ (0.32 lb/ft³), no failures after 48 years for posts treated to 7.8 kg/m³ (0.49 lb/ft³), and one failure (out of 29 posts) after 48 years for posts treated to 3.7 kg/m³ (0.23 lb/ft³). However, it should be noted that all of the post studies mentioned here appear to have been conducted with round posts which have a treatable outer band of sapwood. Jack pine has moderately low strength and moderately low shrinkage.

### White Pine (Eastern)

Eastern white pine (*P. strobus*) is an important timber species in Wisconsin but is not currently used for sign posts. Its

primary current uses are pulpwood and lumber, and it has moderate value relative to other Wisconsin species (Fig. 13). Wisconsin's white pine appears to be a somewhat "underutilized" resource as annual growth is currently almost four times annual removals (Table 3). Eastern white pine wood

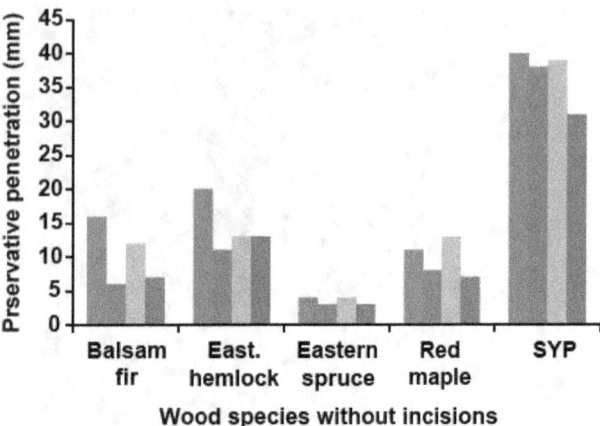

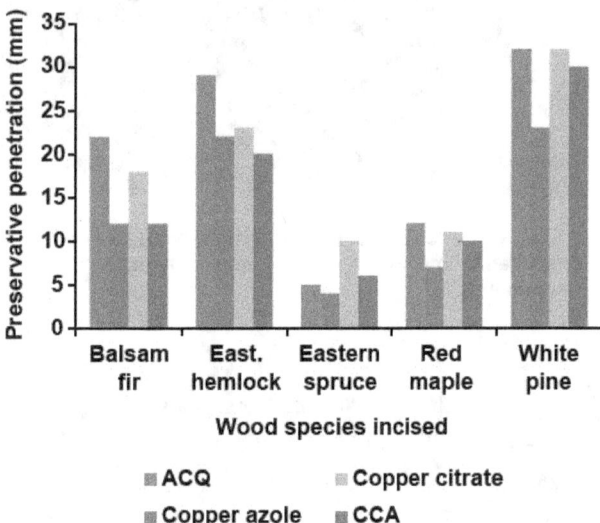

**Figure 14. Preservative penetration in unincised or incised northeastern wood species treated one of four types of preservatives. Adapted from Lebow et al. 2005a.**

has relatively low in strength, and it has never been widely used for preservative treatment. Perhaps because of the lack of use it has a somewhat unusual classification within AWPA standards. Despite its apparent treatability, incising is required for treatment with all preservatives except CCA. The exception was made for CCA when a treating company in the Northeastern United States provided AWPA with data demonstrating eastern white pine's treatability with that preservative. Because CCA is not exceptional in its ability to penetrate during treatment, it appears likely that incising would not be needed for at least some other preservatives as well, but those changes have not been made to the standards. Smith (1986) also found eastern white pine to be readily treated and questioned the need for incising in AWPA standards. Treatability evaluations at FPL indicate that although penetration in eastern white pine is not equivalent to that in Southern Pine, it is at least as great as that in red pine and

greater than that in other Wisconsin species (Figs. 11, 14).

Durability data for 2 by 4 (nominal) stakes exposed at FPL's test site in southern Mississippi also indicates that treated eastern white pine is similar in durability to treated red pine, with or without incising (Table 4). Canadian researchers also report the durability of white pine, with no failures in 20 posts thermally treated with creosote after 71 years of exposure in Ontario, Canada (Morris and Ingram 2010). An advantage of eastern white pine is its relatively low shrinkage and high dimensional stability. Given its combination of growth volume in Wisconsin, treatability with preservatives, and good dimensional stability, eastern white pine appears to be a potential candidate species for use in sign posts.

### Douglas-Fir

Douglas-fir (*Pseudotsuga menziesii*) is not native to, but can be grown in, Wisconsin. Preservative-treated Douglas-fir is widely used for structural elements, particularly in western states. Douglas-fir's large size, straight growth, and relatively high strength (for a softwood) make it particularly useful for large timbers and poles. From a treatment perspective, Douglas-fir is characterized by a relatively narrow sapwood band and a high proportion of difficult to treat heartwood. Because of this treatment difficulty, incising is required for Douglas-fir, and some preservatives (such CCA) are not recommended. Preservatives commonly used to treat Douglas-fir include the ammoniacal formulations (i.e., ACZA and ACQ-B) as well as the oil-type formulations. Treatment schedules for Douglas-fir also tend to be substantially longer than those for pine species. Douglas-fir grown in drier climates and higher elevations tends to be less treatable than that grown along the west coast, and some specifications limit the use of Douglas-fir to that from coastal areas. The durability of adequately treated Douglas-fir has been well established through years of in-service performance as well as with some test data. However, much of the in-service durability of Douglas-fir has been documented with round utility poles, which have an intact outer band of treatable sapwood. There is less documentation of the durability of sawn Douglas-fir, although research at Oregon State University indicates that durability is excellent when incised and treated with effective preservatives (Morrell et al. 1999). Square posts incised and treated with a creosote–oil mixture have had no failures after 57 years. Unincised square posts treated with precursors of CCA or ACZA had average lives of 36 and 33 years, respectively.

### Western Larch

Western larch (*Larix occidentalis*) is not native to Wisconsin, and primarily grows in eastern Oregon and Washington, western Montana, and northern Idaho. Although not as common or as widely used, western larch has similarities to Douglas-fir and the two species are sometimes grouped in the Douglas-fir–Larch species group. The wood is moderately stiff and strong, but does have moderately high shrinkage.

**Table 4. Condition of ACA- or CCA-treated 38- by 89-mm (2- by 4-in. nominal) stakes after 24 years in southern Mississippi. The AWPA specified ground-contact retention for ACZA and CCA is 6.4 kg/m$^3$ (0.4 lb/ft$^3$) for normal use and 9.6 kg/m$^3$ (0.6 lb/ft$^3$) for critical structures.**

| Wood species | Incised? | ACA-treated stakes | | | CCA-treated stakes | | |
|---|---|---|---|---|---|---|---|
| | | Retention (kg/m$^3$) | Some decay (%) | Failed (%) | Retention (kg/m$^3$)[a] | Some decay (%) | Failed (%) |
| Eastern white pine | No | 4.16 | 100 | 100 | 4.96 | 30 | 0 |
| Eastern white pine | No | 6.72 | 100 | 44 | 7.04 | 0 | 0 |
| Eastern white pine | No | 11.52 | 10 | 10 | 10.4 | 0 | 0 |
| Eastern white pine | Yes | 4.16 | 100 | 50 | 5.28 | 22 | 0 |
| Eastern white pine | Yes | 6.72 | 89 | 22 | 8.32 | 0 | 0 |
| Eastern white pine | Yes | 11.68 | 0 | 0 | 11.84 | 0 | 0 |
| Red pine | No | 4.64 | 100 | 100 | 3.68 | 90 | 40 |
| Red pine | No | 4.8 | 100 | 67 | 5.12 | 44 | 22 |
| Red pine | No | 7.04 | 11 | 0 | 7.36 | 11 | 0 |
| Red pine | Yes | 4.96 | 90 | 70 | 4 | 60 | 0 |
| Red pine | Yes | 6.4 | 67 | 11 | 6.4 | 0 | 0 |
| Red pine | Yes | 10.24 | 22 | 0 | 8.8 | 0 | 0 |
| Eastern spruce | No | 2.56 | 100 | 100 | 2.24 | 100 | 80 |
| Eastern spruce | No | 4 | 100 | 100 | 3.2 | 70 | 50 |
| Eastern spruce | No | 6.24 | 100 | 50 | 11.36 | 0 | 0 |
| Eastern spruce | Yes | 3.84 | 90 | 80 | | | |
| Eastern spruce | Yes | 4.48 | 100 | 70 | | Not tested | |
| Eastern spruce | Yes | 7.68 | 20 | 0 | | | |
| Balsam fir | No | 4.16 | 100 | 100 | | | |
| Balsam fir | No | 5.12 | 100 | 67 | | Not tested | |
| Balsam fir | No | 9.44 | 0 | 0 | | | |
| Balsam fir | Yes | 4.64 | 100 | 33 | | | |
| Balsam fir | Yes | 6.4 | 40 | 20 | | Not tested | |
| Balsam fir | Yes | 11.68 | 0 | 0 | | | |
| Eastern hemlock | No | 3.2 | 100 | 100 | | | |
| Eastern hemlock | No | 5.12 | 100 | 60 | | Not tested | |
| Eastern hemlock | No | 5.92 | 30 | 0 | | | |
| Eastern hemlock | Yes | 5.44 | 100 | 62 | | | |
| Eastern hemlock | Yes | 6.08 | 10 | 0 | | Not tested | |
| Eastern hemlock | Yes | 10.88 | 0 | 0 | | | |

Like Douglas-fir, western larch has a large, difficult to treat heartwood, and in it is often considered even more difficult to treat than Douglas-fir. With the notable exception of utility pole cross-arms, western larch is not listed in the AWPA sawn lumber and timbers standards. However, it is listed for use in round posts, poles, and piles that maintain an outer layer of treatable sapwood. In general, there has been relatively little research on either the treatability or durability of western larch. Field exposure data for western larch tends to reflect older preservatives and treatment methods, making it difficult to determine if the lack of treatability or the preservative efficacy controlled durability. However, it is notable that posts pressure-treated with creosote had an average life of only 20 years when exposed in Mississippi, while those pressure-treated with zinc chloride lasted an average of only 15 years in Wisconsin (Gjovik and Davidson 1975). Post treated by steeping with either mercuric chloride or sodium fluoride were more durable than the pressure-treated posts, with average lives of 39 or 28 years (respectively) when exposed in Wisconsin. All of these posts were round, however, and thus should have had an outer layer of treatable sapwood.

### Hem-Fir

Hem-Fir is a species grouping that includes western hemlock (*Tsuga heterophylla*), red fir (*Abies magnifica*), grand fir (*A. grandis*), noble fir (*A. procera*), white fir (*A. concolor*) and Pacific silver fir (*A. Amabilis*). The native range of these species is the Pacific coast from northern California up into Alaska. The species are characterized by light-colored, light weight wood with little obvious color differentiation between sapwood and heartwood. The group has moderate strength and shrinkage that varies from low to moderately high. The largest component of the grouping is typically western hemlock. As with other species groupings, the Hem-Fir grouping appears to have developed somewhat out of convenience because the species, sometimes grown in mixed stands, are difficult to differentiate once milled, and have somewhat similar properties. However, there can be a substantial difference in mechanical properties and treatability between the species. Although species in the Hem-Fir grouping tend to be somewhat more treatable than the Douglas-fir grown in the same region, they are less treatable than pine species and incising of all species in the grouping is required by AWPA standards. There is relatively little durability data on many of the true firs in the Hem-Fir grouping, although some data are available for western hemlock (see western hemlock heading in this section). In general, care should be taken in the use of this species grouping for sign posts as the properties of the posts may vary depending on the species mix.

### Western Hemlock

Western hemlock (*Tsuga heterophylla*) is often included within the Hem-Fir species grouping and typically represents the largest proportion of that grouping. The natural range of western hemlock is along the Pacific coast from Oregon north to Alaska, although some does occur in northern Idaho. It is a relatively large and common tree, making it second only to Douglas-fir in economic importance in that region. Western hemlock has moderate strength and moderately high shrinkage. It typically has a narrow sapwood band, but the differentiation between sapwood and heartwood is not always visible once the wood has dried. Although more treatable than Douglas-fir, treatability of western hemlock is variable between trees and within a single board, and incising is required by AWPA standards. In many cases, western hemlock can be treated adequately enough to be durable without incising; researchers at Oregon State University report that unincised sawn western hemlock posts treated with precursors of CCA or ACZA had average lives of 49 and 32 years, respectively (Morrell et al. 1999). However, incising should increase average durability as well as decreasing the likelihood of early failure.

### Oaks (Red and White)

The current WisDOT specification does not differentiate among oak species. There are numerous oak species in Wisconsin and additional species in other states, but for the purposes of this report we will group those species under the broad categories of red and white oak. Red oaks are generally somewhat treatable with preservatives but have rela-

tively low natural durability. In contrast, white oaks are very resistant to preservative treatment but have moderately high natural durability. In Wisconsin, red, black, and pin oak are examples of red oaks, whereas white, burr, and swamp oak are examples of white oaks. Both red and white oaks occur in substantial volume in Wisconsin, although there is a substantially greater volume of red than white oaks (Table 3).

### Red Oaks

Red oaks (*Quercus* spp.) are an important resource in Wisconsin with both substantial growth volume and substantial removals for commercial use. Red oaks are among the most valuable of Wisconsin species (Fig. 13), with much of the higher quality red oak used for saw logs and veneer, where the monetary values obtained are likely to greatly exceed that obtained for sign post products. A large volume is also used for firewood, but it is likely that much of this volume is derived from small stems and branches, or from lower value large trees. The potential value of red oak for other applications and its growth form may make it challenging to obtain the dimensions needed for sign posts at costs similar to those for currently paid for softwood species. Red oak is stronger than other species listed in Wisconsin DOT signpost specifications, but does exhibit fairly high shrinkage. Red oak species are listed in AWPA standards for a variety of uses, including sawn posts. The most common use for treated red oak is railroad ties, but treated timbers are also sometimes used for bridge construction. Research indicates that red oak is moderately treatable (Crawford et al. 2000; Laks et al. 1996); it is less treatable maple or pine but more treatable than white oaks. Once adequately treated, red oak is durable, although, like other hardwoods, it tends to be somewhat less durable than softwoods when treated with water-based preservatives (Fig. 15). Hardwoods are more commonly treated with oil-type preservatives such as creosote, pentachlorophenol, and copper naphthenate. The durability of red oak is similar to that of Southern Pine when treated with creosote (Fig. 16).

### White Oaks

Although white oaks (*Quercus* spp.) do not occur in as great abundance as red oaks, they remain an important species mix in Wisconsin. Like red oak, the larger and higher quality logs are valuable when used for lumber and veneer production (Fig. 13), but much of the volume is used for firewood. Also like red oaks, white oak wood is strong but undergoes moderately high shrinkage during drying. In the context of preservative treatment and durability, the major difference between white and red oak is the presence of tyloses in the vessels of white oak. The tyloses hinder fluid flow within the wood, making white oak difficult to treat but also causing it to be much more durable than red oak. White oak is listed in AWPA standards, but its use is generally limited to railroad ties. In deference to poor treatability, it is the only species group in which AWPA standards still allow "treatment to refusal" as a measure of treatment

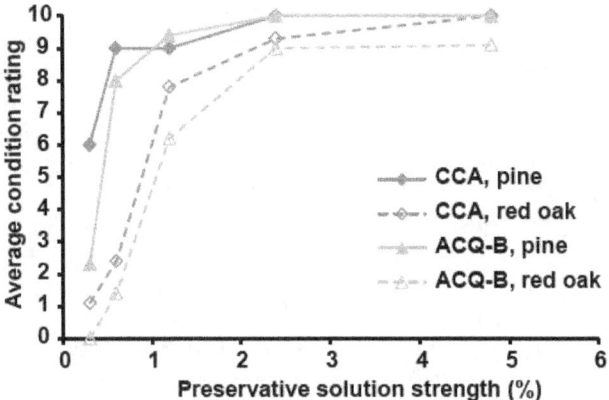

**Figure 15. Comparison of the condition or Southern Pine and red oak stakes after treatment with water-based preservatives and 11 years of exposure in southern Mississippi.**

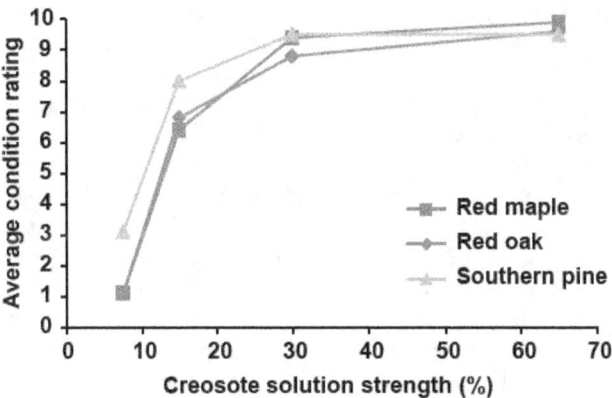

**Figure 16. Comparison of the condition of red maple, red oak, and Southern Pine stakes after treatment with creosote and 9 years of exposure in southern Mississippi.**

quality rather than specifying minimum penetration and retention requirements. However, a recent proposal to AWPA by the manufacturers of the preservative ACZA included data showing that some penetration in white oak is possible, albeit to a lesser extent than red oak. Their proposal, which was subsequently adopted by the AWPA, does call for minimum penetration and retention specifications when white oak is treated with ACZA. There is relatively little information on the durability of pressure-treated white oak. However, one study did find that white oak posts thermally treated (a non-pressure method) with creosote had an average life of 37 years when exposed in Maryland. Other durability evaluations with non-pressure treatments of white oak posts produced less impressive results, with average lives ranging from 13 to 29 years (Gjovik and Davidson 1975).

## Treatability and Durability of Other Wisconsin Wood Species

One of the objectives of this report is to review the potential for increased use of Wisconsin wood species for sign

posts. Use of locally sourced wood for sign posts decreases transportation costs and may also provide benefit Wisconsin land-owners and industries. Currently red pine is the only Wisconsin wood species frequently used for sign posts, although white pine and oak are also allowed under the specification. In this section, the treatability and durability of Wisconsin wood species not currently included in the sign post specification are reviewed for their possible use as sign posts. Species were selected for review based on their classification as a major Wisconsin wood species by the Wisconsin Department of Natural Resources (Table 3).

## Ash

Wisconsin has a significant ash resource, with white (*Fraxinus Americana*), black (*F. nigra*) and green (*F. pennsylvanica*) ash all present in the state. The volume of ash growth each year is also approximately four times greater than that harvested (Table 3), indicating that ash could be available for sign posts without conflicting with existing types of utilization. As of 2012, ash had moderate commercial value (Fig. 13), but those data may not reflect the recent increase in ash removal in anticipation of the potential for infestation by the invasive emerald ash borer. This devastating insect has been associated with high ash mortality in states where it has become established. Currently emerald ash borers have been detected in several Wisconsin counties, and widespread infestation appears inevitable. In the near term, ash availability is expected to increase as local governments begin to remove and replace ash trees in anticipation of future infestation. There is great interest in finding ways to utilize these trees (Brashaw et al. 2012) and the City of Madison, Wisconsin, recently expressed interest in renting a portable sawmill (WSJ 2012) so that the ash trees removed could be utilized for wood products other than chips. In the much longer term, however, availability of ash wood could decline substantially if the emerald ash borer becomes widely established.

Ash has not traditionally been used for durable applications and has relatively little natural durability. Pressure-treated ash is occasionally used for railroad ties as part of a mixed species grouping, but there is little use of preservative-treated ash in other applications. However, the little information that is available does indicate that ash is somewhat treatable. Early researchers at FPL conducted creosote treatments of 25 hardwood species and grouped them into three categories based on extent of creosote penetration (Teesdale and MacLean 1918). Both green and white ash were placed into the most treatable category. Subsequently, Tesoro et al. (1966) compared the extent of creosote penetration and retention in nine hardwoods and six softwoods, and found that ash was more treatable than many species, although greater penetration and retention was observed for maple. Koch (1985) reviewed data on uptake of creosote or pentachlorophenol solution by a range of hardwood species with non-pressure treatments and found that ash was among the most treatable species. The exception to this relatively positive portrayal of ash treatability was as an evaluation of the pressure treatment of a 22 hardwood species with a pentachlorophenol solution (Koch 1985). In that study, green ash fell in the middle in terms of treatability, while white ash ranked in the lower third.

There are a little data on the durability of preservative-treated ash. The average life of treated green ash fence posts has been reported to range from 12–30 years, while two trials with white ash noted average lives of 11 and 21 years (Blew and Kulp 1964). Durability varied depending on preservative, method of application, and severity of exposure site; none of the posts used in these tests were pressure-treated.

## Aspen

Wisconsin has two native species of aspen: quaking (*Populus tremuloides*) and bigtooth (*P. grandidentata*) aspen. Aspen has one of the highest growth volumes in Wisconsin, but is currently being utilized at a higher rate than it is being replenished (Table 3). Aspen traditionally has not been used for durable wood products and information on its treatability and subsequent durability is limited. Like other North American hardwoods, it theoretically would be allowed for use in railroad ties under AWPA's "Mixed Hardwoods" category, but such use would be unusual. Aspen has little natural durability and must be preservative treated for outdoor applications (Blew and Kulp 1964). Research that has been conducted with quaking aspen indicates that its treatability can vary substantially both within and between pieces (Cooper 1976; Kaufert 1948; Mackes and Lynch 2001). The sapwood is reported to be treatable (Smith 1986) and it has been recommended that treatments focus on small diameter younger trees that have greater proportion of sapwood (Wengert 1985). Cooper (1976) reported that heartwood in some pieces was also treatable, and that heartwood treatability appeared to be a function of geographic source. It should be noted that Cooper (1976) used relatively rigorous treatment conditions (heated solution and 3- to 20-h pressure periods) that could be considered onerous by treating plants more accustomed to treating pine species. It has also been reported that small dimensions are more treatable than large dimensions, and that sawn lumber treats more consistently than round stock (Kaufert 1948). Kaufert attributed the latter observation to the exposure of cell lumens on the wood surface during milling, but it is probable that this effect is attributable to more uniform drying of smaller dimension material. Aspen wood can contain "wet pockets" that have much higher moisture content than the surrounding wood and resist drying (Mackes and Lynch 2001; Wengert 1985). Some of the variability in aspen treatability is likely a result of these wet pockets interfering with preservative flow. The literature indicates that effective treatment of aspen may be possible after thorough drying, although a rigorous quality control process would be necessary to account for variability in treatment.

Much of the data on durability of preservative-treated quaking aspen are based on posts treated by non-pressure methods or with preservatives that are no longer in use or both. Blew and Kulp (1964) report average lives for treated aspen posts ranging from as little as 6 years to as much as 37 years in Wisconsin. The latter was achieved with a creosote retention of 150 kg/m$^3$ (9.4 lb/ft$^3$), which is similar to that currently specified for pressure treatment of posts. Posts treated with water-based zinc chloride to a retention of 21 kg/m$^3$ (1.32 lb/ft$^3$) were nearly as durable, with an average life of 33 years (zinc chloride is no longer used as a wood preservative). Blew and Kulp (1964) also report on one test with bigtooth aspen posts, noting that they had an average life of 15 years after cold-soaking in a pentachlorophenol solution. In general, the post data do indicate that aspen posts can be quite durable if adequately treated.

## Balsam Fir

Balsam fir (*Abies balsamea*) is a relatively minor species in Wisconsin, and its utilization volume is currently nearly equivalent to its growth volume (Table 3). When judged solely on availability, balsam fir does not appear to be an ideal candidate for production of large volumes of sign posts. Research also indicates that balsam fir is somewhat resistant to preservative penetration. Gjovik and Schumann (1992) found that incising was required to obtain adequate penetration of CCA in balsam fir, although penetration was substantially better with ACA (Fig. 11). As a note of explanation, Gjovik and Schumann intentionally selected red pine and white pine specimens with substantial heartwood, and thus penetration in these pine species was less than might be expected for sapwood. Lebow et al. (2005b) also reported poor penetration of CCA and copper from another water-based preservative (CuBor) in balsam-fir (Fig. 17). Penetration of boron was much greater, but the boron in current formulations is leachable and would not provide long-term protection for sign posts. Poor treatability with CCA was again confirmed in another study of the treatability of northeastern species (Lebow et al. 2005a), but this study also indicated that better penetration was possible with ACQ (Fig. 14). Improved treatment was achieved with incising, but still lagged well below that of Southern Pine.

As part of their evaluation of northeastern species, Gjovik and Schumann (1992) installed sets of 38 by 89 by 457 mm (2 by 4 by 18 in. nominal) treated stakes in FPL's test site within Harrison Experimental Forest in southern Mississippi (Table 4). For balsam fir, only ACA-treated stakes were included in the tests. These stakes have been evaluated for their extent of decay and insect attack for 24 years. The ACA-treated balsam fir stakes have been durable when treated to above the AWPA UC4A retention (6.4 kg/m$^3$) for ACA (ACZA) general-use posts, but two stakes treated to 6.4 kg/m$^3$ have failed. None of the stakes treated to higher retentions suffered significant attack, even when treated without first incising the wood. It is worth

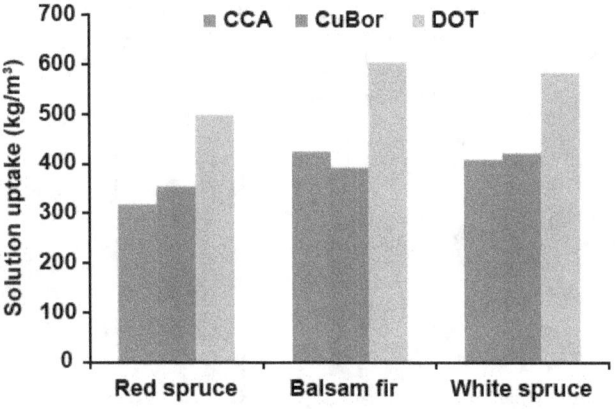

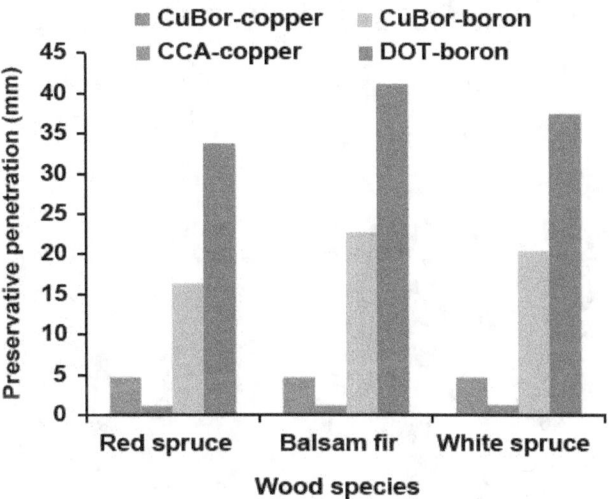

Figure 17. Preservative uptake and penetration in unincised spruce or balsam-fir. Adapted from Lebow et al. 2005b.

noting that for eastern spruce, which was treated with both ACA and CCA in this study, stakes treated with CCA appeared to be more durable than those treated with ACA (Table 4) even though preservative penetration was greater with ACA (Fig. 11). This may indicate that balsam fir stakes would also have been more durable if treated with CCA.

## Basswood

There is an intermediate volume of basswood (*Tilia americana*) in Wisconsin, and currently the volume of growth is approximately twice that utilized (Table 3). Like aspen, basswood has very little natural durability. Also like aspen, basswood is technically allowed for use in railroad ties under AWPA's "Mixed Hardwoods" category, but such use is not typical. There appears to have been little interest in the preservative-treatment of basswood, with the exception of on-site treatment of fence posts in the first half of the 20th century. The research that is available generally indicates that basswood is treatable, at least when pressure-treated. Teesdale and MacLean (1918) included basswood among

the most treatable of three groups of hardwoods when pressure-treated with creosote, and a high retention was achieved when round basswood fence posts were pressure-treated with creosote (Gjovik and Davidson 1975). Tesoro et al. (1966) also found that creosote penetration in basswood heartwood was among the highest of the mixed hardwood and sapwood species he evaluated. Research on treatability of basswood by non-pressure means is less conclusive. Mac-Donald (1915) reported that creosote uptake by basswood posts during thermal treatment was good, but that transverse (across the grain) penetration was only about 8 mm (1/3 in.). Blew (1961) also noted that penetration of basswood during cold-soaking was primarily through the end-grain, and that satisfactory treatment could only be obtained on relatively short pieces. Canadian researchers reported substantial uptake with thermal treatment, although penetration data was not provided (Kulp 1966). Gjovik and Davidson (1975) reported intermediate non-pressure preservative uptake in basswood posts when compared with other species evaluated.

When adequately treated, basswood can be quite durable. Posts pressure-treated to a high retention with creosote-solvent solution had no failures after 56 years in test in Wisconsin, while posts treated by non-pressure means (and with lower retentions) had average lives ranging from 5.4 to 32 years (Gjovik and Davidson 1975). The lower durability appears to be for posts that were only treated on one end. MacDonald (1915) estimated that basswood posts soaked in creosote would last an average of 25–30 years, although this estimate appears to be based on an exposure period of less than 10 years.

## Birch—Paper and Yellow

Although there is a substantial volume of birch in Wisconsin, the growth volume is low in comparison to the volume currently used (Table 3). This is particularly true for paper birch (*Betula papyrifera*), for which annual removal currently greatly exceeds annual growth. Neither paper nor yellow birch (*B. alleghaniensis*) is naturally durable, and historically there has been little interest in preservative treatment of birch, and particularly paper birch, because of its value in other applications. Teesdale and MacLean (1918) did evaluate the treatability of yellow birch with creosote and placed it into the most treatable group of the species they evaluated. More recently, FPL researchers pressure-treated yellow birch heartwood stakes (19 by 19 by 457 mm) with either CCA or ACQ as part of a larger durability evaluation. Uptake by the yellow birch stakes was similar to that of Southern Pine (Fig. 18), but caution is warranted in interpreting these results because of the small specimen dimensions. Paper birch posts have been subjected to preservative treatment by non-pressure methods. Gjovik and Davidson (1975) report that paper birch posts immersed in a pentachlorophenol/diesel solution obtained uptakes ranging from 11.2 kg/m³ (1.7 lb/ft³) to 107 kg/m³ (6.7 lb/ft³) for

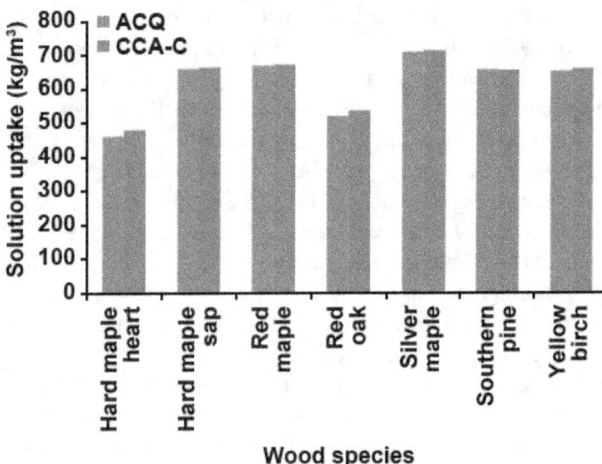

Figure 18. Uptake of preservative by 19- by 19- by 457-mm (0.75- by 0.75- by 18-in.) stakes during pressure treatment. Note that the small dimension of these stakes tends to minimize species differences.

immersion periods ranging from 8 to 168 h. Blew (1961) conducted cold-soak treatments with a range of species and concluded that paper birch was characterized by adequate end-grain penetration but minimal penetration across the grain.

Much of the long-term durability data available for birch is for fence posts that were treated without pressure. Yellow birch posts soaked for 48 h in a creosote–oil solution had average lives in Mississippi of 8 years without incising but 20 years if the lower portion was incised before treatment, presumably because the incisions increased preservative penetration and uptake (Gjovik and Davidson 1975). White birch posts soaked in a 5% pentachlorophenol–oil solution for 8 to 168 h had average lives ranging from 4 to 16 years when exposed in southern Mississippi, while those soaked for 48 h lasted an average of 20 years in Wisconsin. In a separate study, sets of white birch posts soaked in a 5% pentachlorophenol–oil solution had averages lives ranging from 16 to 29 years when installed in Minnesota (Kulp 1966). Longer service (over 32 years) was reported for white birch posts thermally treated with creosote and place in test in Ontario, Canada (Kulp 1966). More recently, FPL researchers evaluated the durability of 19- by 19-mm (¾- by ¾-in.) yellow birch stakes treated with a range of preservatives as part of a larger durability evaluation (Fig. 19). After 11 years exposure in southern Mississippi, it appears that the yellow birch stakes are less durable than Southern Pine stakes when compared at equivalent solution concentrations. However, durability equivalent to Southern Pine was observed for the highest concentration (2.4%) of ACQ-B.

## Eastern Hemlock

Both the existing and growth volume of eastern hemlock (*Tsuga canadensis*) in Wisconsin is less than that of many

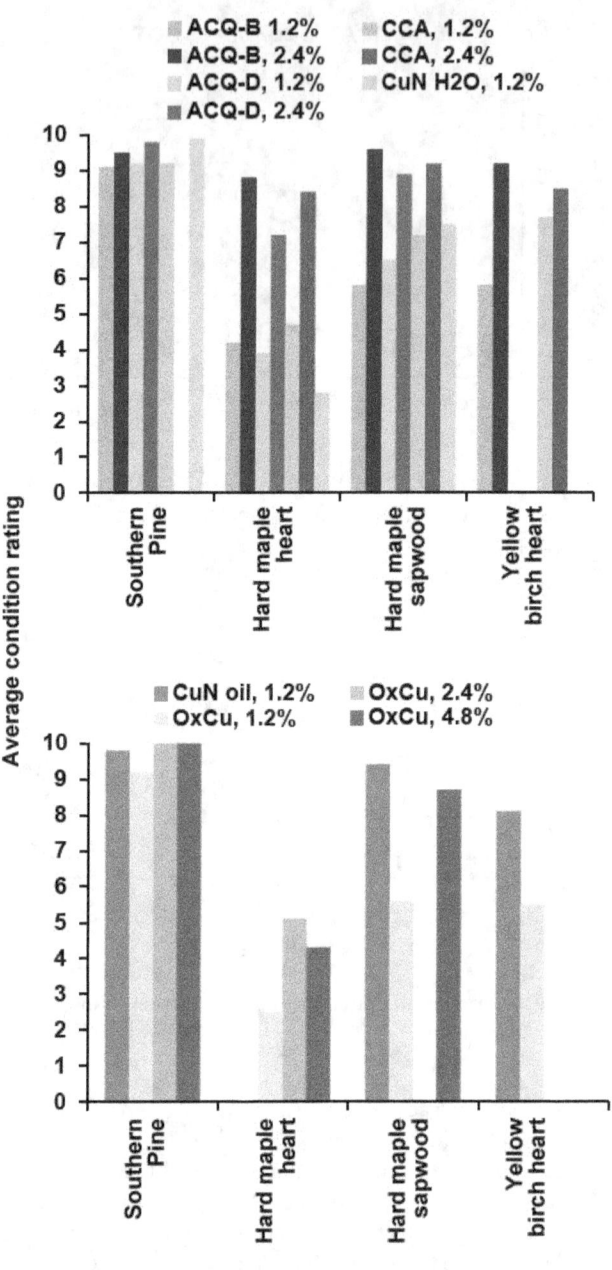

Figure 19. Average condition of 19- by 19- by 457-mm (0.75- by 0.75- by 18-in.) treated stakes after 11 years exposure in southern Mississippi. Upper graph and lower graphs show water-based and oil-based treatments, respectively. Some bars are absent because not all combinations were tested.

other major species. However, it is also the least utilized of major Wisconsin species (Table 3). The size and form of older eastern hemlock trees would allow milling of relatively long posts. Eastern hemlock is moderately low in strength, but also moderately low in shrinkage. Eastern hemlock has not been favored for lumber production because the wood is coarse and uneven in texture, and tends to splinter when cut or drilled. However, a greater disadvantage relative to use in sign posts is the tendency of eastern hemlock trees to suffer from "ring shake." Ring shake is a condition where the wood separates longitudinally parallel to the annual growth rings. Strength can be substantially impacted when this occurs. Eastern hemlock is included in AWPA standards for treated sawn products, but incising is required. Studies on the treatability of eastern hemlock have produced somewhat varying results. Gjovik and Schumann (1992) found that treatability of eastern hemlock was less than that of other northeastern species unless incised (Fig. 11), whereas Smith (1986) found eastern hemlock to be fairly treatable even without incising. Lebow et al. (2005a) reported poor penetration in eastern hemlock without incising, but much better penetration after incising (Fig. 14).

Relatively little long-term data exist on the durability of treated eastern hemlock. However, exposure tests of 2 by 4 (nominal) stakes in southern Mississippi indicate that eastern hemlock stakes treated with ACA (precursor to ACZA) are at least as durable as those of other northeastern species when treated to similar retentions (Table 4). Incised stakes had higher ACA retentions and were more durable.

## Elm

Although common in southern Wisconsin, American (*Ulmus americana*), slippery (*U. rubra*), and rock (*U. thomasii*) elm species represent a relatively minor proportion of Wisconsin's major timber species. In Wisconsin, elm is currently used primarily for firewood and pulpwood, with relatively little lumber production. Elm has value in veneer production (for furniture), but the prevalence of Dutch elm disease prevents most trees from reaching merchantable size. Elm has moderately high strength and shrinkage. Elm has little natural durability, and there is little evidence of its use with preservative treatment. However, like other hardwoods it may be a component of the "mixed hardwoods" grouping allowed for treatment of railroad ties (AWPA 2013). The limited research available on preservative treatment of elm species indicates that they are at least moderately treatable. Teesdale and Maclean (1918) grouped American and slippery elm with the most treatable species for pressure treatment with creosote, and classified rock elm as moderately treatable. American elm was also among the most treatable hardwood species for pressure or thermal treatment with pentachlorophenol, but only moderately treatable by cold-soaking with pentachlorophenol or water-based solutions (Koch 1985). The durability data for elm species is inconclusive. Non-pressure treatments with pentachlorophenol formulations provided only moderate or even low protection of round posts, but the retentions were relatively low. Pressure and thermal treatments with creosote yielded higher retentions and no failures after 18 (Mississippi) or 12 (Wisconsin) years, but inspections on these posts were discontinued (Gjovik and Davidson 1975). However, split posts

thermally treated with creosote to only 48 kg/m$^3$ (3.0 lb/ft$^3$) lasted an average of 32 years in Minnesota.

## Maples, Hard

Sugar (*Acer saccharum*) and black (*A. nigrum*) hard maples are among the most abundant of Wisconsin timber species, although not as abundant as the soft maples discussed below. Despite their value in pulp, furniture, and flooring production, as well as high stumpage prices, the annual growth of hard maples in Wisconsin greatly exceeds the annual harvest. Hard maples are high in strength, moderately high in shrinkage, and have no natural durability. Hard maples have limited use with preservative treatments, but the maple genus (*Acer* spp.) is listed in AWPA Commodity Specification A (Sawn Products) for use above ground as well as for general-use ground-contact applications (including sign posts). However, creosote is the only preservative currently standardized for treatment of the maple species.

There is relatively little treatability information that is specific to hard maples. Teesdale and Maclean (1918) evaluated the treatability of sugar maple with creosote and placed it in the "intermediate" category. FPL researchers treated 19- by 19-mm (¾- by ¾-in.) hard (sugar) maple specimens with ACQ and CCA as part of a durability evaluation and found that while uptake in the sapwood stakes was similar to other species, uptake in hard maple heartwood was diminished (Fig. 18). Kamdem and Chow (1999) treated similar size specimens of sugar maple, red maple, red oak, and beech with copper naphthenate and CCA. They found no statistical difference in treatability between sugar maple and red maple, but did note that in some cases the maples had significantly greater retention than red oak or beech.

Note, however, that the small dimensions of specimens in both studies may have minimized treatment differences between species. Because hard maple species tend to have a relatively thick sapwood band, it is likely that sawn products from these species will have a substantial proportion of the more treatable sapwood.

There is also relatively little information on the durability of hard maple species following pressure treatment with preservatives. The data that are available appear to be limited to relatively small specimens. FPL researchers compared the durability of hard maple sapwood and heartwood to that of Southern Pine and yellow birch heartwood following treatment with a range of water or oil-based preservatives (Fig. 19). The results indicate that treated hard maple sapwood is more durable than treated hard maple heartwood, possibly because of the lower solution uptake by the latter during treatment. It is also apparent that treated hard maple is less durable than treated Southern Pine when compared at lower treatment solution concentrations (Fig. 19). A possible exception to this trend is the relatively equivalent durability of hard maple sapwood and Southern Pine when treated with oil-borne copper naphthenate.

## Maples, Soft

The Wisconsin soft maple wood species are primarily red (*A. rubrum*) and silver (*A. saccharinum*), with red maple comprising over 85% of the growth volume. This species grouping has the greatest growth volume as well as the highest proportion of "unused" growth volume of any species grouping in Wisconsin (Table 3). The wood of the soft maples is not as strong as the hard maples, but still stronger than Wisconsin's softwood species. The soft maples have moderate shrinkage (less than that of the hard maples). Like the hard maples, soft maples have little natural durability. Soft maples are primarily used for pulpwood, although some are used for veneer production and firewood. Their sawlog value is not as great as the hard maples, but well above that of most softwood species (Fig. 13). There has been some interest in the preservative treatment and use of red maple following an initiative in the 1990s to find value-added application for underutilized wood species in the northeastern United States. As part of this effort, red maple was added to AWPA standards as a species for use in the production of glulam timbers. Currently only creosote formulations are standardized for treatment of red maple glulams.

Studies of the treatability of soft maple species have produced conflicting results. Teesdale and MacLean (1918) placed silver maple sapwood into the most treatable grouping and silver maple heartwood into the moderately treatable category following pressure treatment with creosote. Koch (1985) reports that studies found red maple to be relatively well-treated with pentachlorophenol by either pressure or non-pressure means. A study of the feasibility of using red maple and yellow poplar lumber for glulam beams noted excellent penetration of creosote into the red maple lumber. Penetration exceeded 2 in., and the uptake of creosote solution in red maple was approximately two times greater than that in red oak (Baileys et al. 1994). Kamdem and Chow (1999) reported red maple to be as least as treatable, and sometimes more treatable, than red oak when treated with copper naphthenate or CCA, and FPL researchers found that in small stakes, uptake of ACQ and CCA in silver maple and red maple was similar to that of Southern Pine (Fig. 18). However, studies using slightly larger specimens have indicated that red maple does not treat as well as Southern Pine, eastern white pine, or eastern hemlock (Crawford et al. 2000; Lebow et al. 2005a) (Fig. 14).

The relative durability of treated soft maple appears to differ with type of preservative. FPL researchers found red maple to be as durable as Southern Pine or red oak when treated with creosote (Fig. 16), but less durable than Southern Pine when treated with water-based preservatives (Fig. 20). This is similar to the findings noted for hard maple and to those reported by Slahor et al. 2001 and Lebow et al. 2010. These findings help to explain why maple species are currently only standardized by AWPA for treatment with creosote. These studies do indicate, however, that red maple can be

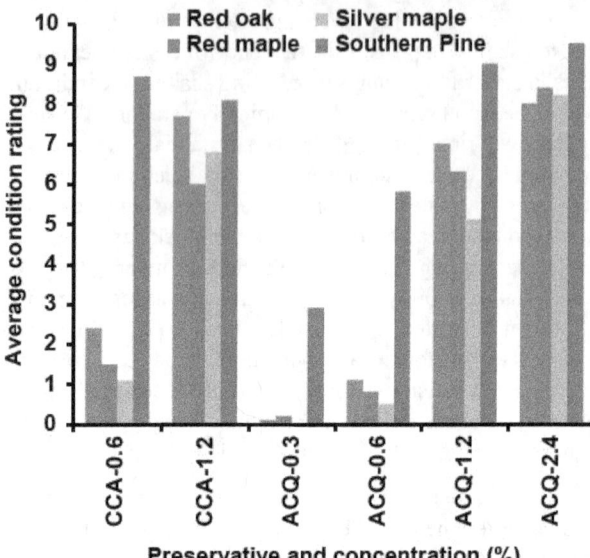

Figure 20. Durability of 19- by 19- by 457-mm (0.75- by 0.75- by 18-in.) stakes of several species after treatment with ACQ or CCA and 11 years of exposure in Mississippi.

as durable as Southern Pine if treated with higher concentrations of water-based preservatives.

## Spruce

White (*Picea glauca*) and black (*P. mariana*) spruce are relatively minor commercial timber species in Wisconsin and grow primarily in the northern third of the state. For commercial use, black and white spruce are often not distinguished from the red spruce (*P. rubens*) found in the northeastern United States, and the three combined species are called eastern spruce. Spruce is primarily used for pulpwood in Wisconsin, although it does have some value for saw logs. The estimated value of spruce logs differs substantially whether determined by the State of Wisconsin methods or industry survey (Fig. 13). Spruce wood has moderately low strength, moderate shrinkage, and little natural durability. White and black spruce are included in the Spruce–Pine–Fir species mix within AWPA standards and thus are standardized for use above ground and when treated with ACQ, ACZA, or borates. This listing does not include ground-contact applications such as sign posts. However, black spruce is also included in the Spruce–Pine–Fir (West) species group, which does allow use in ground contact (including sign posts) when treated with ACQ, ACZA, or CCA. With one exception, AWPA standards require that spruce species be incised prior to treatment to achieve sufficient penetration. The exception applies to borate treatment of wood to be used indoors.

Both white and black spruce are considered relatively resistant to preservative treatment. As with balsam fir and eastern hemlock, the sapwood and heartwood of the spruces species are difficult to distinguish once the wood has dried.

One laboratory evaluation of white spruce heartwood found that an average of 25% to 42% (depending on the moisture content) of the cross section was penetrated following pressure treatment with CCA (Cech et al. 1974). In their study of the treatability and durability of refractory species, Richards and Inwards (1989) reported that white spruce was among the most difficult to treat species, although trees obtained from one geographic area in Canada were more treatable. A subsequent laboratory evaluation of lumber sections found that both white and red spruce were very resistant to preservative treatment with CCA (Fig. 17, Lebow et al. 2005b). A larger scale study of black spruce reported that it could be treated to AWPA standards if incised at a density of 9,500 incisions/m² (883 incisions/ft²) and pressed for over 4 h with a heated treatment solution (Hosli and Zahora 1996). Some evaluations of spruce treatability simply refer to "eastern spruce" and do not distinguish the individual species. One such study indicates that the treatability of eastern spruce is similar to that of eastern hemlock or balsam fir, but less than that of eastern white pine (Fig. 11) (Gjovik and Schumann 1992). However, a more recent study found that eastern spruce was less treatable than balsam fir and eastern hemlock (Lebow et al. 2005b). In general, both white and black spruce should be considered difficult to treat, and adequate treatment will require incising.

The difficulty of treating spruce also appears to affect its durability. In their evaluation of 38- by 89-mm (2- by 4-in. nominal) ACA- or CCA-treated stakes in Mississippi, Gjovik and Schumann (1975) observed numerous failures in spruce stakes but many of these stakes were treated to lower retentions than other species. The treated spruce stakes appeared nearly as durable as other species at comparable retentions, and the CCA-treated stakes appeared to be more durable than the ACA-treated stakes. A subsequent study with smaller stakes also found eastern spruce to be one of the least durable species, but again this effect appeared to at least partly relate to retention differences (Lebow et al. 2010). Richards and McNamara (1997) noted little deterioration in 38- by 140-mm (2- by 6-in. nominal) white spruce stakes treated with CCA and exposed for 8 years in Florida. Some of those stakes were treated to relatively low overall retentions, but probably had much higher retentions near the surface because of the poor penetration. Stake tests can sometimes underestimate the risks associated with poor penetration because there are fewer breaks in the treated shell than would typically occur with wood in service. In general, these studies indicate that spruce can be durable if adequately treated.

# Engineering Properties of Wisconsin Wood Species

## Common Mechanical Properties

Common mechanical properties, at 12% moisture content, for various woods are summarized in Table 5 (Kretschmann

2010). The following is a brief description of these properties. The values reported were obtained from small, clear specimens of wood taken from the corresponding tree species. They do not represent structural design values for a specific grade of timber; hence, they should not be used directly for design. However, they can be used for comparing the potential performance of products from one species of wood with another. Further information on the design specifications for wooden signposts can be found in Section 9 of the Standard Specifications for Structural Supports for Highway Signs, Luminaires, and Traffic Signals (AASHTO 2013).

Note that wood density significantly influences mechanical properties of wood products. In general, denser woods have higher mechanical properties (higher density woods are generally stronger than lower density woods). Examination of Table 5 reveals that species having densities similar to or greater than those currently used for signposts have mechanical properties that are comparable.

## Modulus of Elasticity (MOE)

Elasticity implies that deformations produced by low stress are completely recoverable after loads are removed. When loaded to higher stress levels, plastic deformation or failure occurs. The three moduli of elasticity are the elastic moduli along the longitudinal, radial, and tangential axes of wood. These moduli are usually obtained from compression tests.

The modulus of elasticity determined from bending may be the only modulus of elasticity available for a species. Average MOE values obtained from bending tests are given in the attached table. As tabulated, MOE values include an effect of shear deflection; MOE values from bending can be increased by 10% to remove this effect approximately.

## Modulus of Rupture (MOR)

Reflects the maximum load-carrying capacity of a member in bending and is proportional to maximum moment borne by the specimen. Modulus of rupture is an accepted criterion of strength, although it is not a true stress because the formula by which it is computed is valid only to the elastic limit.

## Impact Bending (Impact)

In the impact bending test, a hammer of given weight is dropped upon a beam from successively increased heights until rupture occurs or the beam deflects 152 mm (6 in.) or more. The height of the maximum drop, or the drop that causes failure, is a comparative value that represents the ability of wood to absorb shocks that cause stresses beyond the proportional limit.

## Work to Maximum Load in Bending (WML)

Work to maximum load in bending represents the ability to absorb shock with some permanent deformation and more or less injury to a specimen. Work to maximum load is a

**Table 5. Mechanical properties of Wisconsin species in comparison to Southern Pine and Douglas-fir**

| | | | Clear wood properties[a] | | | |
|---|---|---|---|---|---|---|
| | | Specific gravity | Modulus of elasticity ($\times 10^6$ lb/in$^2$) | Modulus of rupture (lb/in$^2$) | Impact (in.) | Work to maximum load (in-lbf/in$^3$) |
| Southern Pine | Loblolly | 0.51 | 1.79 | 12,800 | 30 | 10.4 |
| | Slash | 0.59 | 1.98 | 16,300 | na | 13.2 |
| | Longleaf | 0.59 | 1.98 | 14,500 | 34 | 11.8 |
| | Shortleaf | 0.51 | 1.75 | 13,100 | 33 | 11.0 |
| Douglas-fir | Inland | 0.46–0.50 | 1.49–1.83 | 11,900–13,100 | 20–32 | 9.0–10.6 |
| | Coast | 0.48 | 1.95 | 12,400 | 31 | 9.9 |
| **Wisconsin hardwoods** | | | | | | |
| Oak | White | 0.68 | 1.78 | 15,200 | 37 | 14.8 |
| | Northern red | 0.63 | 1.82 | 14,300 | 43 | 14.5 |
| Aspen | Bigtooth | 0.39 | 1.43 | 9,100 | na | 7.7 |
| | Quaking | 0.38 | 1.18 | 8,400 | 21 | 7.6 |
| Maple | Red | 0.54 | 1.64 | 13,400 | 32 | 12.5 |
| | Sugar | 0.63 | 1.83 | 15,800 | 39 | 16.5 |
| Black locust | | 0.69 | 2.05 | 19,400 | 57 | 18.4 |
| Basswood | | 0.37 | 1.46 | 8,700 | 16 | 7.2 |
| Ash | Black | 0.49 | 1.6 | 12,600 | 35 | 14.9 |
| | Green | 0.56 | 1.66 | 14,100 | 32 | 13.4 |
| | White | 0.6 | 1.74 | 15,000 | 43 | 16.6 |
| **Wisconsin softwoods** | | | | | | |
| Eastern white pine | | 0.35 | 1.24 | 8,600 | 18 | 6.8 |
| Balsam fir | | 0.35 | 1.45 | 9,200 | 20 | 5.1 |
| Eastern hemlock | | 0.4 | 1.2 | 8,900 | 21 | 6.8 |
| Red pine | | 0.46 | 1.63 | 11,000 | 26 | 9.9 |
| Black spruce | | 0.42 | 1.61 | 10,800 | 23 | 10.5 |
| White spruce | | 0.36 | 1.43 | 9,400 | 20 | 7.7 |
| Jack pine | | 0.43 | 1.35 | 9,900 | 27 | 8.3 |

[a]1 lb/in$^2$ = 47.880 Pa; 1 in. = 25.4 mm; 1 in-lbf/in$^3$ = 6.89 kJ/m$^3$

measure of the combined strength and toughness of wood under bending stresses.

### Lag Screw Withdrawal Resistance

Lag screws are commonly used because of their convenience, particularly where it would be difficult to fasten a bolt or where a nut on the surface would be objectionable (Rammer 2010). Commonly available lag screws range from about 5.1 to 25.4 mm (0.2 to 1 in.) in diameter and from 25.4 to 406 mm (1 to 16 in.) in length. The length of the threaded part varies with the length of the screw and ranges from 19.0 mm (0.75 in.) with the 25.4- and 31.8-mm (1- and 1.25-in.) screws to half the length for all lengths greater than 254 mm (10 in.). Lag screws have a hexagonal-shaped head and are tightened by a wrench (as opposed to wood screws, which have a slotted head and are tightened by a screw driver). The following equations for withdrawal loads are based on lag screws having a base metal average tensile yield strength of about 310.3 MPa (45,000 lb/in²) and an average ultimate tensile strength of 530.9 MPa (77,000 lb/in²).

The results of withdrawal tests have shown that the maximum direct withdrawal load of lag screws from the side grain of seasoned wood may be computed as follows:

$$p = 8,100G^{3/2}\, D^{3/4}\, L \text{ (inch–pound)}$$

where $p$ is maximum withdrawal load (lb), $D$ shank diameter (in.), $G$ specific gravity of the wood based on oven dry weight and volume at 12% MC, and $L$ length (in.) of penetration of the threaded part. (1 lb = 4.45 N; 1 in. = 25.4 mm.)

Assuming equivalent bolt diameter and penetration, the relative withdrawal resistance of species under consideration for sign post use can be compared on the basis of specific gravity (Table 5). Oaks, black locust, and hard maple species are likely to have the greatest maximum withdrawal loads, whereas white pine and eastern hemlock have the least. Southern Pine and red pine, the species currently utilized, have intermediate specific gravity.

## Moisture Content and Shrinkage

The following section briefly describes several important definitions and characteristics of wood that relate its relationship with moisture (Glass and Zelinka 2010). Green moisture content values and shrinkage characteristics for clear wood from several species are shown in Table 6.

### Green Moisture Content

Green wood is often defined as freshly sawn wood in which the cell walls are completely saturated with water and additional water may reside in the cell lumens. The moisture

**Table 6. Average moisture content and shrinkage of Wisconsin species in comparison with Southern Pine and Douglas-fir**

| Wood species | | Average moisture content of green wood (%) | | Average shrinkage (%) | | |
|---|---|---|---|---|---|---|
| | | Heartwood | Sapwood | Radial | Tangential | Volumetric |
| Southern Pine | Loblolly | 33 | 110 | 4.8 | 7.4 | 12.3 |
| | Slash | NA[a] | NA | 5.4 | 7.6 | 12.1 |
| | Longleaf | 31 | 106 | 5.1 | 7.5 | 12.2 |
| | Shortleaf | 32 | 122 | 4.6 | 7.7 | 12.3 |
| Douglas-fir | Inland | NA | NA | 3.8–4.8 | 6.9–7.5 | 10.7–11.8 |
| | Coast | 37 | 115 | 4.8 | 7.6 | 12.4 |
| **Wisconsin hardwoods** | | | | | | |
| Oak | White | 64 | 78 | 5.6 | 10.5 | 16.3 |
| | Northern red | 80 | 69 | 4 | 8.6 | 13.7 |
| Aspen | Bigtooth | NA | NA | 3.3 | 7.9 | 11.8 |
| | Quaking | 95 | 113 | 3.5 | 6.7 | 11.5 |
| Maple | Red | NA | NA | 4 | 8.2 | 12.6 |
| | Sugar | 65 | 72 | 4.8 | 9.9 | 14.7 |
| Black locust | | NA | NA | 4.6 | 7.2 | 10.2 |
| Basswood | | 81 | 133 | 6.6 | 9.3 | 15.8 |
| Ash | Black | 95 | NA | 5 | 7.8 | 15.2 |
| | Green | NA | 58 | 4.6 | 7.1 | 12.5 |
| | White | 46 | 44 | 4.9 | 7.8 | 13.3 |
| **Wisconsin softwoods** | | | | | | |
| Eastern white pine | | NA | NA | 2.1 | 6.1 | 8.2 |
| Balsam fir | | 88 | 173 | 2.9 | 6.9 | 11.2 |
| Eastern hemlock | | 97 | 119 | 3 | 6.8 | 9.7 |
| Red pine | | 32 | 134 | 3.8 | 7.2 | 11.3 |
| Black spruce | | 52 | 113 | 4.1 | 6.8 | 11.3 |
| White spruce | | NA | NA | NA | NA | NA |
| Jack pine | | NA | NA | 3.7 | 6.6 | 10.3 |

[a]NA is not applicable.

content of green wood can range from about 30% to more than 200%. In green softwoods, the moisture content of sapwood is usually greater than that of heartwood. In green hardwoods, the difference in moisture content between heartwood and sapwood depends on the species. The average moisture content of green heartwood and sapwood of several species is given in Table 6. These values are considered typical, but variation within and between trees is considerable. Variability of green moisture content exists even within individual boards cut from the same tree.

## Shrinkage Values

Wood is dimensionally stable when moisture content is greater than the fiber saturation point. Below the fiber saturation point, wood changes dimension as it gains moisture (swells) or loses moisture (shrinks), because volume of the cell wall depends on the amount of bound water. This shrinking and swelling can result in warping, checking, and splitting of the wood, which in turn can lead to decreased utility of wood products, such as loosening of tool handles, gaps in flooring, or other performance problems. Therefore, it is important that the dimensional stability be understood and considered when a wood product will be exposed to large moisture fluctuations in service.

With respect to dimensional stability, wood is an anisotropic material. It shrinks (and swells) most in the direction of the annual growth rings (tangentially), about half as much across the rings (radially), and only slightly along the grain (longitudinally). The combined effects of radial and tangential shrinkage can distort the shape of wood pieces because of the difference in shrinkage and the curvature of annual rings. The major types of distortion as a result of these effects are illustrated in Figure 21.

### Transverse and Volumetric Shrinkage

Shrinkage values, expressed as a percentage of the green dimension, are listed in Table 6. The shrinkage of wood is affected by a number of variables. In general, greater shrinkage is associated with greater density. The size and shape of a piece of wood can affect shrinkage, and the rate of drying can affect shrinkage for some species. Transverse and volumetric shrinkage variability can be expressed by a coefficient of variation of approximately 15%.

### Longitudinal Shrinkage

Longitudinal shrinkage of wood (shrinkage parallel to the grain) is generally quite small. Average values for shrinkage from green to oven dry are between 0.1% and 0.2% for most

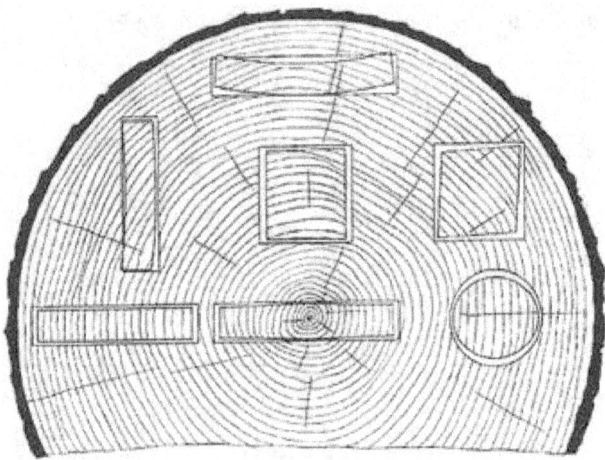

Figure 21. Characteristic shrinkage and distortion of flat, square, and round pieces as affected by direction of growth rings. Tangential shrinkage is about twice as great as tangential. Source: Glass and Zelinka (2010).

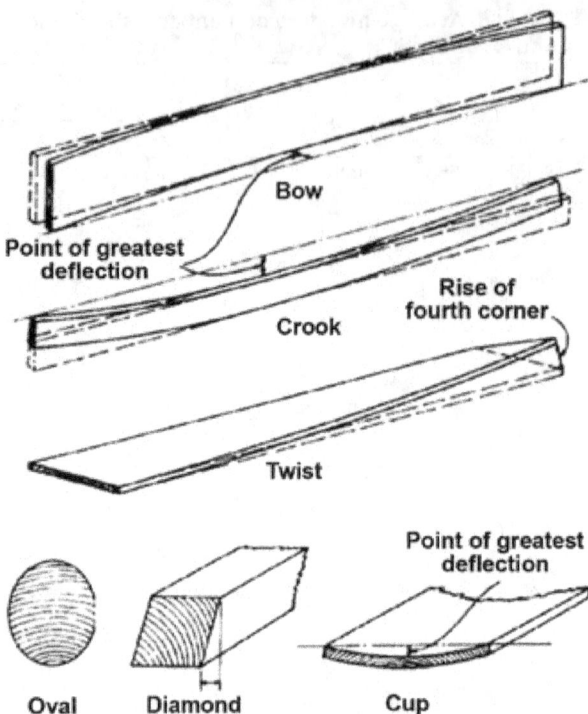

Figure 22. Common types of warp that develop during drying. Source: Simpson (1991).

species of wood. However, certain types of wood exhibit excessive longitudinal shrinkage, and these should be avoided in uses where longitudinal stability is important. Reaction wood, whether compression wood in softwoods or tension wood in hardwoods, tends to shrink excessively parallel to the grain. Wood from near the center of trees (juvenile wood) of some species also shrinks excessively lengthwise. Reaction wood and juvenile wood can shrink 2% from green to oven dry. Wood with cross grain exhibits increased shrinkage along the longitudinal axis of the piece. Reaction wood exhibiting excessive longitudinal shrinkage can occur in the same board with normal wood. The presence of this type of wood, as well as cross grain, can cause serious warping, such as bow, crook, or twist, and cross breaks can develop in the zones of high shrinkage.

## Minimizing Warp in Sign Posts

Warp in wood is caused by differential shrinkage as wood dries. Warp is typically grouped into five categories: bow, crook, twist, diamonding, and cup (Fig. 22) (Simpson 1991). Bow is a deviation from a straight line drawn from end to end on the widest face of a piece of lumber or timber. Crook is similar to bow except that the deviation is edgewise rather than flatwise. Both crook and bow are associated with differential longitudinal shrinkage on opposite faces. Twist is the turning of the four corners of any face of a post so that they are no longer in the same plane. It occurs in wood containing spiral, wavy, diagonal, distorted, or interlocked grain (Simpson 1991). Bow, crook, and twist are the likely the most frequent types of warp in sign posts (Fig. 23). Diamonding is a form of warp found in squares or thick lumber such as sign posts. In a square, the cross section assumes a diamond shape during drying. Diamonding is caused by the difference between radial and tangential shrinkage in

squares in which the growth rings run diagonally (Simpson 1991). Although diamonding can occur in the dimensions used for sign posts, it is not commonly observed in pressure-treated pine. Cup is a deviation across the width of a board causing the edges of the board to be higher than the middle. Although sometimes a problem in treated decking, it is typically not a concern with the dimensions of lumber used in sign posts.

Green sign posts are initially dried (usually in a dry-kiln) under controlled conditions prior to pressure treatment. Some warp may be observed after this initial drying but ideally those pieces would be rejected prior to pressure treatment. Pressure treatment with water-based preservative then re-wets the wood. Moisture contents after treatment with water-based preservatives vary, but are consistently above 30% moisture content. Because nearly all shrinkage occurs as the wood dries below 30% MC, pressure treatment with water-based preservatives does cause subsequent shrinkage and creates and opportunity for warp to occur. Pressure treatment with oil-type preservatives such as creosote, pentachlorophenol, and copper naphthenate does not reintroduce water to the wood, and thus shrinkage and warp is limited to that which occurs when drying the green posts prior to treatment.

Although the extent of shrinkage that occurs does vary by species (Table 6), these differences are relatively small and

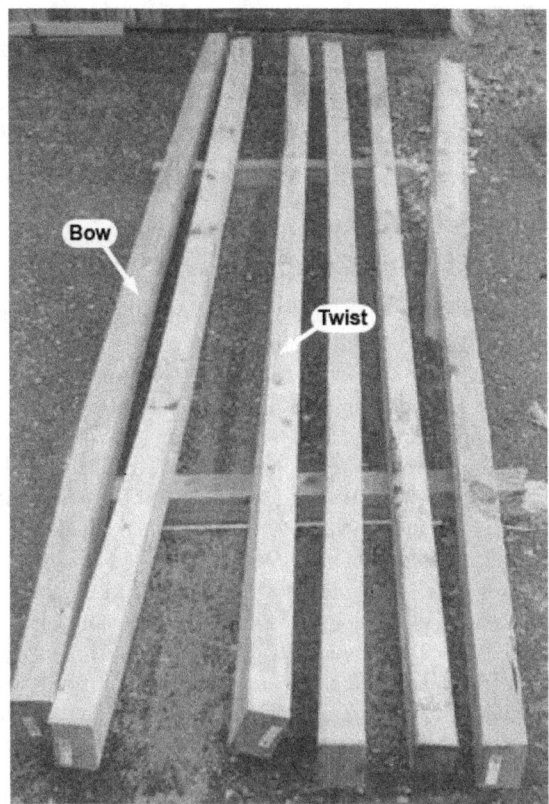

Figure 23. Examples of bow and twist in sign posts. Source: Matt Rauch, WisDOT.

Figure 24. Warp appears to be more common, or at least more visible, in single-post than two-post signs.

not always a good indicator of the potential for warp. Instead, warp is usually associated with wood quality issues within individual pieces. Although the cause of warp is not always obvious, it is often associated with the presences of juvenile wood or reaction wood. When juvenile wood or reaction wood is present on one side of the post but not on the opposite face, the differential in longitudinal shrinkage can cause warp. Growing conditions that create these wood characteristics can be the greatest contributor to warp. In some cases, stands of timber may have an unusually high proportion of reaction wood or juvenile wood. If these trees are sent to single mill, sawed, dried, and then pressure-treated by a single facility, it can create a run of material from that treater with a greater than normal volume of problem pieces. In part because of their length (up to 22 ft (6.7 m)) sign posts are vulnerable to warping as they dry following pressure treatment.

Because wood characteristics are the primary contributor to excessive warp, there is no easy solution to lessening the extent of warp in treated sign posts. Current WisDOT practice is to have the posts stickered after treatment to promote drying and to minimize the time that the posts are exposed horizontally outdoors during storage. Casual observation of in-service WisDOT posts indicates that relatively few have obvious warp, but this does not account for the number of

posts that may have been rejected by WisDOT personnel prior to installation.

A supplier has suggested that WisDOT might experience less warping if the posts were close-stacked after treatment to minimize drying prior to installation. It is unclear if less warp will occur in sign posts if drying and shrinkage occurs after installation, but this type of approach is effective in other applications. Treated deck boards, for example, can be prevented from warping if securely screwed into place prior to drying. However, sign posts are not as thoroughly restrained as deck boards. In two-post signs, some restraint is provided by the ground contact on the bottom end and the sign on the top end. The extent of restraint in this case would depend on the firmness of the post embedment, the length of the posts, and the dimensions of the sign. In single post signs, there is no restraint on the upper end of the post, allowing warp to occur in the length of the post that is above ground (Fig. 24). However, there are at least two other possible mechanisms that could lead to reduced warp in sign posts installed while wet. First, the vertical exposure of a sign post may allow more uniform drying than the horizontal exposure of stacked posts. The outer layers of stacked posts are subjected to differential drying because the outer surfaces are exposed to more airflow than the inner surfaces.

In addition, the upper surface of the top layer of posts may be subjected to direct sunlight while the bottom surface of those posts remains relatively cool. In contrast, in-service sign posts have roughly equivalent air flow to all sides (except the area contacting the sign) and although the sun is likely to hit one or two sides of a post more than others, the angle of the sun is much less extreme. It is also possible that shrinkage would be lessened in installed posts because they would not dry to a moisture content as low. Moisture from the ground is likely to prevent drying in portions of the post near the groundline, while precipitation will keep the upper end of the post moist for a substantial portion of the time. Thus, the length of the post subjected to drying stresses might be substantially reduced. It is important to note, however, that these potential mechanisms of reduced warp are speculative and have not been evaluated.

The most common approach to minimizing warp during drying is the application of physical restraints (Simpson 1991) and reduction of warp by physical restraint during kiln-drying appears to be fairly permanent (Shmulsky 2006). The concept is similar to screwing a deck board securely in place before it dries. In kiln drying, this may be accomplished by placing concrete weights (exerting at least 244 kg/m$^2$ (50 lb/ft$^2$)) on top of the stack in the kiln. This approach is fairly effective at preventing bow or twist, but less effective in preventing crook because the pieces can slide along the stickers. Research indicates that, in combination with top-loading, crook can also be reduced if serrated (toothed) aluminum stickers are used to prevent pieces from sliding on the stickers (Koch 1974). However the use of serrated stickers does not appear to have gained commercial acceptance.

There has been relatively less research on minimizing warp during drying after preservative treatment, but physical restraints may be used in a manner similar to initial kiln-drying. One study noted that warp in CCA-treated Southern Pine 4 by 4s (nominal 3.5 by 3.5 in. (89 by 89 mm) could be significantly reduced by applying pressure with pneumatic cylinders during kiln-drying (Shumlsky 2006). There is also little research on the potential use of physical restraint during air-drying to minimize warp in treated wood, although it is likely to provide a similar benefit. The state of Kansas sign post specification includes the direction to "… *tightly band with spaced layers to permit air flow between each layer and minimize warping. Banding consists of 1 band for each 4 feet of bundle length, with a maximum spacing of four feet between bands, end bands being not more than 1 foot from the end of the bundles. Place spacers (stickers), a minimum of 1/8 inch in thickness, between each horizontal layer of posts at each banding location.*" (KDOT 2007). It is likely that the intent of the banding requirement is to restrain the posts from warping during drying, but it is unclear how effective this approach might be. Once the wood begins to shrink the bands will no longer restrain the wood,

and thus benefit is probably limited to prevention of more extreme cases. Application of a top load might provide additional benefit.

## Other Options: Structural Wood Composites and Naturally Durable Species

### Structural Wood Composites

Structural wood composites are sometimes used as alternatives to solid-sawn wood products. Structural wood composites are lumber, veneers, or strands glued together to form larger, longer members. The most common example is the glulam beams used for both interior and exterior construction. Less common, but still well established in the marketplace, are parallel strand lumber (PSL) and laminated veneer lumber (LVL). All of these structural composites allow the production of wood products that are tailored to dimensions and mechanical properties needed for a specific application. The exterior adhesives allow the composites to be used outdoors, and even in ground contact. Although still a small percentage of the pole market, glulam utility poles are sometimes used in areas where predictable, engineered strength properties are particularly important. The lumber used in glulam posts, poles, and beams can potentially be pressure-treated either before or after gluing. If treated before gluing, water-based preservatives are typically used to minimize interference with adhesive bonding. If treated after gluing, oil-type preservatives are generally used to minimize the drying stresses created by the swelling and shrinking associated with water-based preservatives. PSL is typically treated after gluing and can be treated with water or oil-type preservatives. LVL is only standardized for treatment with creosote after gluing. Southern Pine and Douglas-fir are the woods primarily used in structural composites, although western hemlock, Hem-Fir, red oak, and red maple are also standardized, and in theory, a range of other wood species could also be used.

Structural composites potentially offer several advantages and at least two disadvantages for use in sign posts. In general, the properties of the structural composite posts would be less variable and more predictable than solid sawn posts. They could be engineered to more closely meet strength requirements and it may even be possible to design posts so that drilling of holes to ensure break-away on impact would not be necessary. They would also be less likely to warp than solid sawn posts. It is also possible that a greater range of Wisconsin wood species could be used because it would no longer necessary to obtain 5.5–6.7 m (18–22 ft) long, straight pieces. The primary disadvantage of structural composite posts would be additional cost. A secondary disadvantage would be fewer potential suppliers and more limited availability.

## Naturally Durable Species

Wisconsin has several wood species with some natural durability. The most common of these are black locust (not native and often considered invasive), eastern red cedar (native but sometimes considered invasive), northern white cedar, and white oak. Black locust was widely planted for erosion control by the Civilian Conservation Corps and has since become naturalized. It reproduces vigorously by root suckering and stump sprouting and forms a dense canopy that crowds out native species. Black locust appears to be among the most durable of trees growing in Wisconsin and often grows to sufficient size to obtain the dimensions used for sign posts. However, the trees suffer from attack by a stem borer that can cause deformed growth and reduce the value of the wood. The wood is also difficult to dry without warping. Eastern red cedar and northern white cedar do not appear to be quite as durable black locust, and suffer from variability in their durability. It is uncertain that either of these species would consistently provide a 20+ year service life. In addition, trees of both species are relatively small, making it difficult to obtain the long dimensions needed for posts. Larger trees of both cedar species are also likely to have greater value in other applications. White oak also does not appear to be consistently durable enough to provide the expected service life of sign posts and like cedar, the higher quality wood has greater value in other products. Overall, none of the natural durable species in Wisconsin appear to be ideally suited for use in sign posts. Black locust may have the most potential because of its durability and size, and because it does not as great of value for other applications. However, the supply of suitable black locust posts is likely to be relatively low.

# Summary of Potential Use of Wisconsin Species in Sign Posts

Wisconsin DOT's current use of red pine is a logical choice. Red pine is available in the necessary dimensions, is readily treated with preservatives, has relatively low cost, and has adequate strength properties. Choices among other Wisconsin wood species are less obvious. Although they are not currently being used, Wisconsin DOT's current specification lists jack pine, eastern white pine, and oaks as acceptable species. Jack pine does not appear to be an ideal candidate for use in sign posts. The supply of jack pine in Wisconsin is relatively limited, and it is currently being utilized at a rate that exceeds is growth. Although jack pine is pressure-treated for various applications, it has a relatively thin sapwood band and requires incising to obtain adequate treatment. In contrast, eastern white pine appears to have some potential for use. There is a moderate supply of white pine in Wisconsin, and its rate of growth currently greatly exceeds its utilization. It is also a large tree that should allow mills to obtain posts of the necessary dimensions (Fig. 25). Eastern white pine also appears to be treatable with preservatives, and may

**Figure 25. Eastern white pine's height and form should allow milling to obtain long posts.**

be less prone to warping than red or Southern Pine. The concern with eastern white pine is its relatively low strength. Testing may be needed to determine if eastern white pine is has sufficient strength, especially for longer posts. In contrast, oak species have more than sufficient strength, but have other drawbacks in terms of signpost usage. One of these is cost; oaks have substantial value for other applications and oak posts are likely to be more expensive than pine posts. This is likely to be especially true for the higher quality oak wood. Red oak is moderately treatable, but higher retentions of water-based preservatives may be needed to impart durability. An oil-based preservative such as copper naphthenate may be more appropriate for red oak. White oak is extremely difficult to treat with preservatives, and although it does have some natural durability it is unlikely that it would be consistently durable in ground contact.

Other species of potential interest are the soft maples and ash species. Soft maples are abundant in Wisconsin and their rate of growth greatly exceeds that of their utilization. Soft maple saw timber has moderately high value; less than the oaks but more than that of softwood species. Although not as strong as many other hardwoods, soft maple's strength

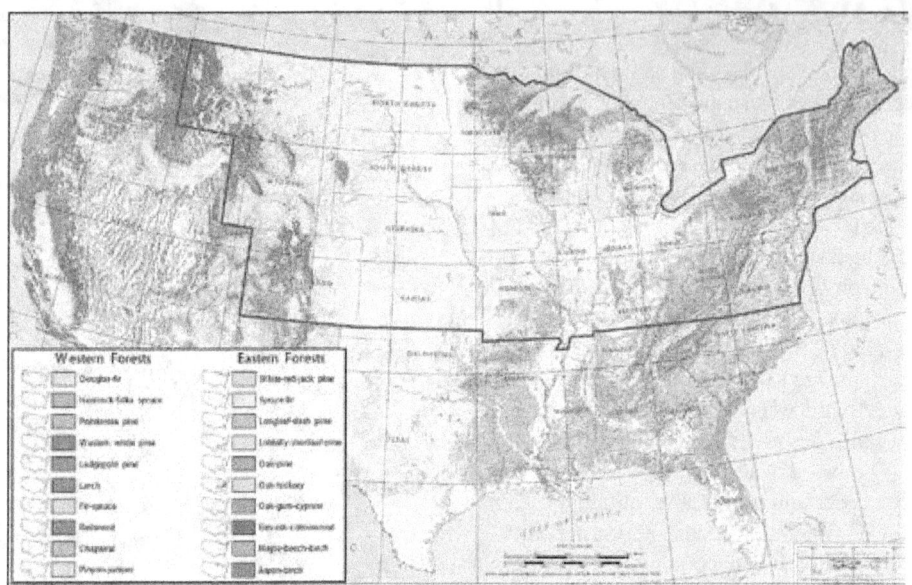

**Figure 26. Major forest types of the lower 48 states. Outlined states were selected for review of highway specifications for wooden signposts. Adapted from *Forest Cover Types, National Atlas of the United States of America*. U.S. Forest Service, Forest Inventory and Analysis, National Office, Arlington, VA. http://www.fia.fs.fed.us/library/ maps/docs/forestcover.pdf**

easily exceeds that needed for sign posts. It also appears to be fairly treatable, although as with other hardwood species it appears to be most durable when treated with oil-based preservatives or higher retentions of water-based preservatives. A concern with the soft maples is whether their growth habit will make it practical to obtain the long-straight dimensions needed for sign posts.

Potential use of ash is interesting because of concerns associated with the emerald ash borer and the increased harvesting of ash by various municipalities. Finding value-added applications for these trees may make their removal more palatable. Ash saw timber currently has moderate value but that may decline as the number of trees harvested to prevent disease increases. There has been relatively little research on the preservative treatment of ash, or its durability once treated. Treatability evaluations may be warranted before pursuing the use of ash sign posts.

Of the species in Wisconsin with natural durability, black locust may have the greatest potential for sign post use. Black locust has sufficient strength and fairly high durability. It is also considered a weedy, potentially invasive species for which removal is often encouraged. However, black locust does have disadvantages for use in sign posts. It is susceptible to insect damage and heartwood decay (in the living tree) and it will be difficult to obtain large volumes of long, straight, defect-free black locust posts.

Structural composite posts suffer little or no warp and could be manufactured to a wide range of dimensions and tailored closely to a targeted end use. They allow use of smaller trees

and could potentially expand the number of useful Wisconsin wood species. However, composites posts are likely to be substantially more expensive than solid-sawn posts, and availability of posts constructed from Wisconsin wood species may be limited.

## Wooden Signage Post Specifications in Other States

One approach to evaluating viable wood species/wood preservative combinations for Wisconsin wooden sign posts is to review the specifications of other states that have some similarities in forest resources. Not surprisingly, neighboring Michigan and Minnesota share the greatest similarity in forest types with Wisconsin (Fig. 26). However, there is some commonality in other Midwestern and northeastern states, and these states were included to expand the survey. Nearby states with relatively little native forest were also included to determine if they were utilizing species from the Great Lakes area. Several eastern Rocky Mountains states were also included to evaluate their possible use of aspen or small-diameter pine species (Fig. 26).

Of the 27 states surveyed, 18 include some form of wooden signposts in their state highway specifications (Table 7). However, one of those states (Ohio) only has specifications for posts constructed from laminated box beams. In addition, no evidence of permanent wooden sign post usage was seen in a Google Street View sampling of 7 of the 18 states that do include wood in their specifications (Table 7). In Colorado, wooden posts were only observed

**Table 7. Wood species and preservatives referenced by states with specifications that include wooden sign posts**

| State | Wood species | Preservative treatment | In use?[a] |
|---|---|---|---|
| Colorado | Douglas-fir (South) or Douglas-fir–Larch[b] | No pressure treatment specified. "*Underground portions of timber sign posts, plus at least 6 inches above groundline, shall be painted with one of the preservatives listed in AASHTO M 13 3* (CDOT 2011)." (Currently copper naphthenate is the only AASHTO M 133 preservative available for brush-on applications.) | No |
| Illinois | Southern Pine, Douglas-fir | AASHTO M 133, Excluding ACQ types B and C and copper azole CA-B and CBA-A | Yes |
| Indiana | Southern Pine, coastal Douglas-fir, catalpa, northern white cedar, eastern and southern red cedar, black locust, yellow locust, mulberry, red, black, and white oak group, osage orange, redwood, sassafras | In accordance with AWPA Standards C14 and C2. Use heavy oil with oil-type preservatives, but post must be paintable | No |
| Iowa | Southern Pine, Douglas-fir | ACZA, CCA, creosote, pentachlorophenol (heavy oil), copper naphthenate (heavy oil) | Yes |
| Kansas | Southern Pine, Douglas-fir | ACA (precursor of ACZA) and CCA[c] | Yes |
| Maine | Southern Pine (treated) or spruce, hemlock, cedar or Douglas-fir | CCA for treatment of southern pine if treated posts are specified. Other species are apparently used untreated in some situations. | Yes |
| Maryland | AASHTO M 168 | AASHTO M 133 | Yes |
| Michigan | Southern Pine, Douglas-fir, balsam-fir, eastern hemlock, eastern white pine, tamarack (eastern larch) | ACZA, CCA, pentachlorophenol. ACQ and copper azole were recently withdrawn from the signpost specification but are still allowed for guardrail posts and blocks. | Yes |
| Missouri | AWPA Standards (general reference)[d] | AASHTO M 133, and also "*other preservatives and wood species in accordance with AWPA Standards* (MODOT 2011)." | Yes |
| Montana | Not specified[e] | ACA (precursor of ACZA), CCA and pentachlorophenol | Yes |
| Nebraska | Coastal Douglas-fir | ACA (precursor of ACZA), ACZA, CCA, pentachlorophenol, or copper naphthenate. Requires re-drying to maximum of 30% moisture content. | Yes |
| New Jersey | Southern Pine, Douglas-fir | CCA or pentachlorophenol (southern pine); ACZA (Douglas-fir) | No |
| Ohio | Laminated veneer box beams | Pentachlorophenol | No |
| Pennsylvania | Southern Pine, Douglas-fir–Larch[b] | ACA (precursor of ACZA), CCA | Yes |
| South Dakota | Coastal Douglas-fir, western larch, western redcedar | ACZA, CCA, pentachlorophenol, copper naphthenate. None required for western redcedar | No |
| Vermont | Oak, cedar, spruce, western fir, or other approved wood | ACQ, CCA, creosote, pentachlorophenol (either light or heavy oil) | No |
| Virginia | Southern Pine | CCA | Yes |
| West Virginia | AASHTO M 168 and structural softwoods meeting (SPIB rules) or hardwoods meeting NELMA structural grades[f] | For softwoods, creosote or water-based preservative listed in AWPA C14 and AWPA P5. Treat hardwoods with water-based preservative according to AWPA C2, excluding CCA (this would include ACC, ACA, ACZA, ACQ, CA-B, and CBA-A) | No |
| Wyoming | Southern Pine, Douglas-fir, lodgepole pine, ponderosa pine | Preservatives listed in AWPA Standard C14 and approved for ground contact. | Yes |

[a]Permanent wooden signposts visible in a Google Street View sampling of state and interstate highways.

[b]"Douglas-fir South" refers to a Western Wood Products Association (WWPA) species group originating from Douglas Fir growing in Arizona, Colorado, Nevada, New Mexico, and Utah. Douglas-fir–Larch refers to a mixture of Douglas-fir and western larch species. In the intermountain west these species are sometimes combined in dimension lumber products because they have similar physical properties.

[c]Also includes this drying instruction: "*Stack and tightly band with spaced layers to permit air flow between each layer and minimize warping. Banding consists of 1 band for each 4 feet of bundle length, with a maximum spacing of four feet between bands, end bands being not more than 1 foot from the end of the bundles. Place spacers (stickers), a minimum of 1/8 inch in thickness, between each horizontal layer of posts at each banding location.*" (KDOT. 2007)

[d]For general posts, AWPA Standards list Douglas-fir, western larch, western hemlock, and six species of pine. Hardwoods and additional softwoods are included under "sawn products."

[e]Other commodities: Allow Douglas-fir, hemlock, ponderosa pine, spruce, larch, or lodgepole pine for guardrail and fence posts, but only Douglas-fir, western larch or southern yellow pine for structural support piles.

[f]Limiting softwoods to Southern Pine Inspection Bureau rules would limit species to Southern Pine group. NELMA stands for Northeastern Lumber Manufacturers Association.

**Table 8. Examples of other preservative-treated wood products specified by states that do not specify wooden sign posts**

| State | Commodities | Wood species | Preservatives |
|---|---|---|---|
| Connecticut | Guard rail posts | Southern Pine or Douglas-fir–Larch[a] | ACZA |
| | Light poles | AWPA C4[b] | CCA, creosote, pentachlorophenol |
| Delaware | Piles, guardrail posts | Southern Pine or Douglas-fir | CCA (creosote was recently withdrawn) |
| Kentucky | Guardrail posts | AWPA C2 (includes many species) | AWPA C14, except creosote only for hardwoods |
| Massachusetts | Guardrail posts | Unclear: implies AWPA standards | ACA (precursor to ACZA) or CCA |
| | Piles | Southern Pine or Douglas-fir | AASHTO M 133 |
| Minnesota | Guardrail posts | Jack pine, red pine, lodgepole pine, ponderosa pine, or Southern Pine | ACA (precursor to ACZA), CCA, creosote, pentachlorophenol (heavy oil) |
| New Hampshire | Guardrail posts | AASHTO M 168 | Pentachlorophenol or water-based meeting preservative meeting AASHTO M 133 |
| New York | Guardrail posts | Treated: Douglas-fir, pine, oak, birch, apple, beech / Untreated: redwood, red cedar, cypress or black locust | ACQ, CA-B or other preservative conforming to AWPA standards (documentation required). CCA is expressly prohibited based on state law. |
| North Dakota | Piles, guardrail posts, piles | Only specify design properties | AASHTO M 133 |
| Rhode Island | Guardrail posts | Spruce or fir | AASHTO M 133 |
| | Piles | Southern Pine or Douglas-fir | AASHTO M 133 |

[a]Douglas-fir–Larch refers to a mixture of Douglas-fir and western larch species. In the intermountain west, these species are sometimes combined in dimension lumber products because they have similar physical properties.
[b]AWPA Standard C4 (Poles) lists Southern Pine, coastal Douglas-fir, jack pine, red pine, lodgepole pine, ponderosa pine, western larch, western redcedar, and Alaska yellow cedar.

as supports for temporary road construction signage. Although this brief sampling does not demonstrate that no wood posts are used in those states, it does indicate that they are used infrequently. No mention of the use of wooden sign posts was found in the specifications of the other nine states surveyed. However, none of these states explicitly prohibit the use of wooden sign posts, and all do allow wood for other structural members in ground contact such as guardrail posts or piles (Table 8).

## Wood Species Referenced by Other States

Many states do not appear to be focusing on the use of local wood species for sign posts. In states that do list specific wood species, Southern Pine and Douglas-fir are the most widely listed even though in most cases those species are not native to the state. It is likely that Southern Pine and Douglas-fir are specified because of familiarity and these species long history of use in structural members. However, some states do include other local species in their specifications. Perhaps the most relevant of these is Michigan, which lists balsam fir, eastern hemlock, eastern white pine, and tamarack (eastern larch) in addition to Southern Pine and Douglas-fir. Colorado does not specify Southern Pine and limits the wood species to Douglas-fir and western larch

species groups that are predominately found in the Rocky Mountain states. Indiana's specification includes a range of local species in addition to Southern Pine, Douglas-fir, and redwood. Although the state of Maine specification requires Southern Pine for treated posts, it also appears to allow use of untreated spruce, hemlock, cedar, and Douglas-fir for some applications. The neighboring state of Vermont does not specify either Southern Pine or Douglas-fir, but instead lists oak, cedar, spruce, and western fir. It is possible that western fir is intended to specify Douglas-fir, although there are several fir species in the western states. South Dakota specifies western larch and western redcedar in addition to coastal Douglas-fir (all non-native species) but somewhat surprisingly does not list the ponderosa pine that is plentiful in the Black Hills region. The state of Wyoming does incorporate native species by listing lodgepole pine and ponderosa pine along with Southern Pine and Douglas-fir. Three states (Maryland, Missouri, and West Virginia) cite either AASHTO M 168 or AWPA standards for allowable species rather than listing individual species.

States that do not specify wood for sign posts also most commonly specify Southern Pine and Douglas-fir for other treated wood commodities (Table 8). A notable

**Figure 27. California uses round poles or large sawn posts to support larger highway signs.**

exception is Minnesota, which does include red pine, jack pine, lodgepole pine, and ponderosa pine in its specification for guardrail posts. New York state also has an expanded list of species for guardrail posts, including pine (no specifics on species), oak, birch, beech, and even apple. They also allow redwood, red cedar, cypress, and black locust as untreated guardrail posts. Rhode Island also allows use of spruce and fir in guardrail posts, but limits pile species to Southern Pine and Douglas-fir. Connecticut cites AWPA Standard C4 for wood species used in light poles, which would appear to allow jack pine, red pine, lodgepole pine, ponderosa pine, western larch, western redcedar, and Alaska yellow cedar.

The highway specifications from other states (Table 7) should be interpreted carefully for their applicability to using alternative Wisconsin wood species for sign posts. Relevant alternative species listed in other states' specifications include balsam fir, eastern hemlock, eastern white pine, oak, spruce, and tamarack (eastern larch), as well as the naturally durable species eastern red cedar and black locust. However, all states except Vermont also include Southern Pine or Douglas-fir in their specification, and it is likely that these two species account for the bulk of their wood sign posts. In other cases, a state may list wooden sign posts in their specification but not actively use them. Communication with staff at Vermont's DOT revealed that they typically do not use wooden sign posts of any species, a finding that agrees with the lack of wooden posts observed in Google Street View. Indiana lists many species but some do not appear to be suitable for production of large volumes of longer sign posts (although perhaps they could be occasionally used for shorter posts), and wooden posts were not observed in a Google Street View sampling of that state's highways. Thus, inclusion of alternatives species in a state's specification does not necessarily indicate that these species (or wood sign posts in

general) are successfully utilized on a consistent basis. Similarly, states that do use wooden sign posts may not use them in the same lengths or for as broad a range of applications as does Wisconsin.

The most relevant specification for comparison appears to that of the state of Michigan. Michigan's specification for wooden signposts is detailed and has been kept current with AWPA Standards. Michigan also includes three wood species (balsam fir, eastern hemlock, and eastern white pine) which are major wood species in Wisconsin (Table 7). However, in response to an inquiry, the Michigan Department of Transportation indicated that their suppliers are generally providing Southern Pine posts, and that their experience with other species is minimal.

Although an examination of California's sign post specification was not included in this review, it is interesting to note that California uses wooden signposts extensively, and for larger signs than either Wisconsin or Michigan (Fig. 27). California uses post dimensions as large as 6 by 10 in. (nominal) or round poles to support larger signs.

## Wood Preservatives Referenced by Other States

A fairly broad range of sign post preservative treatments are allowed by state's highway specifications, with ACZA (ACA) and CCA most frequently specified (Table 7). However, several states also list oil-type treatments, while others refer to AASHTO M 133 or AWPA Standard C14 (Highway Construction) rather than specifying individual preservatives. As shown in Table 9, AASHTO M 133 and AWPA Standard C14 list most of the major ground-contact oil and water-type ground-contact wood preservatives. An important difference between the two standards is that AWPA Standard C14 does not list the most recent version of copper azole (CA-C) or the newer particulate (micronized) copper preservatives that have received evaluation reports from the ICC-ES. Because AWPA Standard C14 was replaced as part of the conversion to the Use Category System, it has not been updated since 2004 and will not be updated in the future. Michigan's specification cites the more current AWPA standard, which does include CA-C, but does not include the micronized copper preservatives because data packets for these preservatives have not been submitted to AWPA for review.

Those states that specify all preservatives in AASHTO M 133 or AWPA Standards (or individually specifying ACA or ACZA) appear to be allowing use of the high-copper preservatives (ACQ, copper azole, ACZA) that are potentially corrosive in contact with aluminum signs. However, because CCA is also allowed under those specifications it is likely that most of their post suppliers have continued to use CCA. It is also possible that these states are taking other steps to minimize corrosion, although such measures are not readily evident in their specifications. The state of Illinois

**Table 9. Sign post applicable preservatives listed in either AASHTO M 133 or AWPA Standard C14[a]**

| Pressure-treatment preservative | Listed by[b] | |
| --- | --- | --- |
| | AASHTO M 133 | AWPA Standard C14 |
| Water-type preservatives | | |
|     Acid copper chromate (ACC) | Yes | Yes |
|     Alkaline copper quat (ACQ) Type B | Yes | Yes |
|     Alkaline copper quat (ACQ) Type C | Yes | Yes |
|     Alkaline copper quat (ACQ) Type D | Yes | No |
|     Ammoniacal copper arsenate (ACA) | No | Yes |
|     Ammoniacal copper zinc arsenate (ACZA) | Yes | Yes |
|     Chromated copper arsenate (CCA) | Yes | Yes |
|     Copper azole Type A (CBA-A) | Yes | Yes |
|     Copper azole Type B (CA-B) | Yes | Yes |
|     Copper azole Type C (CA-C) | Yes | No |
|     Micronized/dispersed) copper azole (MCA or µCA-C) | Yes | No |
|     Micronized copper quat (MCQ) | Yes | No |
| Oil-type preservatives | | |
|     Copper naphthenate | Yes | Yes |
|     Creosote and creosote solutions | Yes | Yes |
|     Pentachlorophenol (heavy or light oil) | Yes | Yes |

[a]States that do not specify wood for sign posts do specify similar preservatives for other treated wood commodities (Table 8). Most commonly these states reference AASHTO M 133, but ACZA, CCA, creosote, and pentachlorophenol are also individually specified. However, two of these states expressly exclude either creosote (Delaware) or CCA (New York). The prohibition on use of CCA in New York appears to be based on general state policy rather than concerns about the risks associated with use of CCA-treated wood in highway construction. ACQ and copper azole are suggested alternatives, but it should be noted that New York does not use wooden sign posts and thus contact with aluminum is less of a concern. In Delaware, removal of creosote from the specification appears to derive from concerns about the potential environmental impact of treated wood placed into aquatic environments (i.e., bridge piles).
[b]From the 2010 version of AASHTO M 133 and the 2004 (last) version of AWPA Standard C14. AWPA Standard C14 is no longer being updated because AWPA converted to the Use Category System.

is an exception in that it does specify AASHTO M 133, but specifically excludes ACQ and copper azole formulations, presumably because of corrosion concerns. Similarly, Michigan specifies use of ACZA, CCA, or pentachlorophenol but specifically excludes use of ACQ and copper azole for sign posts even though those preservatives are allowed for guardrail posts. Michigan also adds a footnote: "Non-Metallic washers or spacers are required for timber and lumber treated with ACQ or CA placed in direct contact with aluminum (MDOT. 2012)." Currently, the suppliers to Michigan DOT are primarily providing sign posts treated with CCA (personal communication on February 19, 2013, with Steven Kahl, Supervising Engineer, Michigan Department of Transportation, Lansing, Michigan.)

There appears to be little attempt to minimize use of the conventional "heavy duty" preservatives ACZA, CCA, creosote, and pentachlorophenol preservatives in state sign post specifications. This may in part reflect that some of the specifications have not been updated recently (as evidenced by specifying ACA and AWPA Standard C14) but even the more current specifications include the heavy duty preservatives. The extent of human contact is low for highway sign posts in comparison to some construction applications, and this may have lessened perceived health concerns associated with the older preservatives.

# Summary

## Preservatives and Wood Species

WisDOT's current practice of using red pine or Southern Pine posts treated with CCA is logical and may be the optimum combination of wood species and preservatives currently available. Red pine and Southern Pine are readily available wood species with relatively large and treatable sapwood zones. They are also relatively strong compared with many other softwood species. Pressure-treated Southern Pine is widely used for structural purposes, including for sign posts by other states. Use of red pine is more geographically limited, but it is an important local resource and a logical choice for use in Wisconsin. The use of CCA wood preservative is also a logical choice. CCA is an effective preservative with a long track record and is compatible with aluminum signs. Although CCA does contain arsenic, and is a RUP, it is still commonly used for treatment of utility poles, marine piles, and bridge timbers. It also appears to be the preservative most widely used by other states for treatment of sign posts. A potential disadvantage of CCA is that it does not appear to protect hardwoods species as well as it does softwood species. If WisDOT begins utilizing hardwood species for sign posts, it may be necessary to either increase the CCA retention requirement or specify that the hardwoods be treated with an oil-type preservative.

## Considerations for Alternative Preservatives

Potential alternatives to CCA fall into two categories: water-based preservatives and oil-based preservatives. The water-based preservatives that are suitable for sign posts rely primarily on copper for efficacy and appear to present an increased risk of corrosion of the aluminum signs. The particulate copper systems that have become widely used in residential decking are marketed as having increased compatibility with aluminum, but may still be more corrosive than CCA. The particulate copper systems are also less able to penetrate difficult to treat wood species than water-soluble preservatives. Thus, there are no obvious alternatives to CCA among the current water-based preservatives. Because compatibility with aluminum is the greatest obstacle to using copper-based wood preservatives, it may be desirable to evaluate additional approaches to isolating the sign from the post.

All of the common oil-type preservatives (creosote, copper naphthenate, and pentachlorophenol) would effectively protect sign posts from decay, and all have the additional advantage of compatibility with aluminum. In addition, they are effective in protecting both softwood and hardwood species, and are likely to diminish the occurrence of warp in the sign posts. However, creosote and pentachlorophenol are RUPs, and thus would not overcome potential toxicity concerns associated with CCA. Copper naphthenate is not a RUP and may be a reasonable alternative to CCA. It does, however, have a noticeable odor and wood may initially have an oily surface.

## Considerations for Alternative (Wisconsin) Wood Species

In addition to red pine, WisDOT's current specification lists jack pine, eastern white pine, and oaks as acceptable Wisconsin species. The supply of jack pine in Wisconsin is relatively limited, and it has a relatively thin sapwood band and requires incising to obtain adequate treatment. Eastern white pine is available in larger volumes, appears to be treatable with preservatives, and may be less prone to warping than red or Southern Pine. However, white pine may not have sufficient strength for sign posts. In contrast, oak species have more than sufficient strength, but the long, straight dimensions needed for sign posts are likely to have much greater value in other applications. In addition, white oak is difficult to treat with preservatives.

Additional species of interest not currently listed in WisDOT specifications are the soft maples and ash. Soft maples are abundant in Wisconsin and their rate of growth greatly exceeds that of their utilization.

Soft maple also appears to be fairly treatable, although as with other hardwood species they appear to be most durable when treated with oil-based preservatives or higher retentions of water-based preservatives. A concern with the soft maples is whether their growth habit will make it practical

to obtain the long-straight dimensions needed for sign posts. Ash is currently being harvested by various local governments in anticipation of emerald ash borer infestation and there is interest in finding value-added applications for these trees. However, there is relatively little experience with ash treatability and durability, or its susceptibility to warp when used in long dimensions. In general, the supply of sign posts from alternative Wisconsin wood species might be expected to be more limited and less consistent than that of red pine. However, it may be possible to increase use of alternative species by focusing their use on shorter posts or posts with lesser strength requirements.

WisDOT's current use of red pine or Southern Pine posts treated with CCA may be the optimum combination of wood species–preservative currently available. Continued use of this combination is recommended unless/until CCA and/or these wood species become unavailable and WisDOT choses to purchase posts of one or more hardwood species (in which case an oil-type preservative would be more appropriate).

Copper naphthenate in oil solvent appears to be one of the most logical alternative wood preservatives to use instead of CCA. However, wood treated with copper naphthenate has some odor and may initially have a somewhat of oily surface. WisDOT may want to consider purchasing a small volume of copper naphthenate-treated posts to evaluate their handling characteristics. Copper naphthenate is less widely used than CCA, and there are currently no pressure-treatment facilities in Wisconsin using copper naphthenate.

Of Wisconsin tree species, red pine appears to be best suited for use in sign posts, and its continued use is recommended. Other Wisconsin species are likely to be either less readily available in necessary dimensions, less treatable with preservatives, lacking in needed strength properties, or more costly. If use of other Wisconsin species becomes a priority, species to consider include the following:

- Eastern white pine, which is already allowed under WisDOT specifications. Strength may be a concern with this species.

- Soft (red and silver) maple, which are not currently in WisDOT specifications but which grow in relatively large volumes in Wisconsin and are relatively underutilized. Cost, availability in needed dimensions, and warp may be considerations with these species.

- No clear-cut solution was identified for reducing the incidence of warp in sign posts, although it is likely that warp could be reduced by use of an oil-type preservative. The most effective approach to minimizing warp during drying appears to be physical restraint of the stickered stack of posts during drying. Such physical restraint may be impractical to employ on a routine basis, but WisDOT may want to consider placing weights (such as concrete traffic barriers) on some stacks of drying posts to evaluate this option. WisDOT may also want to consider installing some posts while still wet as suggested by a supplier. These posts would need to be identified and monitored for future evaluation of warp development. Ideally they would be compared with posts from the same supplier shipment that had been dried before installation. When posts are stacked outdoors to dry, direct contact of sunlight on the outer surface of the upper layer of posts could cause more rapid drying on that face and contribute to increased drying stresses and warp. The practice of drying posts indoors should help to minimize this problem and should be continued. If posts are dried outdoors, it may be worthwhile to cover the upper surface to protect it from direct sunlight and rainfall. For example, sheets of plywood could be placed on stack of posts (with additional stickers between the posts and the plywood).

# References

AASHTO. 2013. Section 9. Wood design. In: Standard Specifications for structural supports for highway signs, luminaires, and traffic signals. Sixth Edition. Washington, D.C.: American Association of State Highway and Transportation Officials. 289 p.

Anthony Forest Products. n.d. Copper naphthenate corrosivity data. El Dorado, AR: Anthony Forest Products Company. http://www.anthonyforest.com/pdfs/cunap_corrosivity.pdf . Accessed April 1, 2013.

AWPA. 2007. AWPA E-12: Standard method of determining corrosion of metal in contact with treated wood. Standard published 01/01/1994 by American Wood Protection Association (formerly the American Wood-Preservers' Association). Birmingham, AL: American Wood Protection Association. 1 p.

AWPA. 2012. Book of Standards. Birmingham, AL: American Wood Protection Association. 644 p.

Baileys, R.T.; Webb, D.A.; Blankenhorn, P.R.; Janowiak, J.J.; Labosky, P.L.; Kessler, K.R.; Kilmer, W.R.; Manbeck, H.B.; Schaffer, K.R. 1994. Hardwood glulam and creosote treatment–an evaluation of gluebond performance and structural strength characteristics. Proceedings, 90th Annual Meeting of the American Wood Preservers Association. May 14–18, San Antonio, TX. pp. 128–135.

Baker, A.J. 1992. Corrosion of nails in CCA- and ACA-treated wood in two environments. Forest Products Journal. 42:39–41.

Blew, J.O. 1961. Treating wood by the cold-soaking method. Report No. 1445. Madison, WI: U.S. Department of Agriculture, Forest Service, Forest Products Laboratory. 20 p.

Blew, J.O.; Kulp, J.W. 1964. Service records on treated and untreated fence posts. Res. Note FPL–068. Madison, WI: U.S. Department of Agriculture, Forest Service, Forest Products Laboratory. 53 p.

Brashaw, B.K., Ross, R.J., Wang, X.; Wiemann, M.C. 2012. Wood utilization options for urban trees infested by invasive species. Madison, WI: Forest Products Society. 82 p.

CDOT. 2011. Standard Specifications for Road and Bridge Construction. Division 600, Miscellaneous Construction. Colorado Department of Transportation. http://www.coloradodot.info/business/designsupport/construction-specifications/2011-Specs/2011-specs-book

Cech, M.Y.; Pfaff, F. 1974. CCA retention and disproportioning in white spruce. Forest Products Journal. 24(7): 26–32.

Clausen, C.A. 2010. Biodeterioration of wood. In: Wood handbook–wood as an engineering material. R. Ross, ed. General Technical Report FPL–GTR–190. Madison, WI: U.S. Department of Agriculture, Forest Service, Forest Products Laboratory: 14-1–14-16. Chapter 14.

Cooper, P.A. 1976. Pressure-preservative treatment of poplar lumber. Forest Products Journal. 26(7):28–31.

Crawford, D.M.; De Groot, R.C.; Watkins, J. B.; Greaves, H.; Schmalzl, K.J.; Syers, T.L. 2000. Treatability of U.S. wood species with pigment emulsified creosote. Forest Products Journal. 50(1): 29–35.

Davidson, H.L. 1977. Comparison of wood preservatives in Mississippi post study (1977 progress report). Research Note FPL–RN–01, Madison, WI: U.S. Department of Agriculture, Forest Service, Forest Products Laboratory, 18 p.

Freeman, M.H.; Crawford, D.M.; Lebow, P.K.; Brient, J.A. 2006. A comparison of wood preservatives in posts in southern Mississippi: results from a half-decade of testing. Proceedings, 101st Annual Meeting of the American Wood-Preservers' Association. May 15–17, 2005, New Orleans, LA. 101, 136–143.

Freeman, M.H.; McIntyre, C.R. 2008 A comprehensive review of copper-based wood preservatives with a focus on new micronized or dispersed copper systems, Forest Products Journal. 58:6–27.

Gjovik, L.R.; Davidson, H. L. 1975. Service records on treated and untreated fence posts. USDA, Forest Service Research Note FPL-068. Madison, WI: U.S. Department of Agriculture, Forest Service, Forest Products Laboratory. 44 p.

Gjovik, L.R.; Schumann, D.R. 1992. Treatability of native softwood species of the northeastern United States. Res. Pap. FPL–RP–508. Madison, WI: U.S. Department of Agriculture, Forest Service, Forest Products Laboratory. 20 p.

Glass, S.V.; Zelinka, S.L. 2010. Moisture relations and physical properties of wood. In: Wood Handbook–Wood as an Engineering Material. Ross, R., ed. General Technical Report FPL–GTR–190. Madison, WI: U.S. Department of Agriculture, Forest Service, Forest Products Laboratory: Pp. 4-1–4-19. Chapter 4.

Hosli, J.P.; Zahora, A.R. 1996. Wood preservative treatment of Newfoundland black spruce. FPD Report No. 80. Forest Products & Development Division, Newfoundland Forest Service. Corner Brook, NF. 16 p. http://www.nr.gov nl.ca/nr/publications/forestry/tech_reports/FPD_Report_80.pdf

Kamdem, D.P.; Chow, P. 1999. The effect of pressure on retention and bending properties of copper naphthenate and CCA Type C treated hardwoods. Wood and Fiber Science. 31(2):1288–135.

Kaufert, F.H. 1948. Preservative treatment of aspen. Lake States Aspen Report No. 19. USDA, Forest Service, Lake States Experiment Station. 19 p.

KDOT. 2007. Standard Specifications for State Road and Bridge Construction (2007). Section 2301, Wood Posts. Kansas Department of Transportation. https://www.ksdot.org/burconsmain/specprov/2007SSDefault.asp

Kear, G.; Wu, H.-Z.; Jones, M.S. 2009. Weight loss studies of fastener materials corrosion in contact with timbers treated with copper azole and alkaline copper quaternary compounds. Corrosion Science. 51:252–262.

Knotkova-Cermakova, D.; Vlckova, J. 1971. Corrosive effect of plastics, rubber and wood on metals in confined spaces. British Corrosion Journal. 6:17–22.

Koch, P. 1974. Serrated kiln sticks and top load substantially reduce warp in Southern Pine studs dried at 240 F. Forest Products Journal. 24(11):30–34.

Koch, P. 1985. Utilization of hardwoods growing on southern pine sites–Volume 2. Agricultural Handbook SFES-AH-605. Asheville, NC: USDA Forest Service, Southern Forest Experiment Station. 1419–2542.

Kretschmann, D.E. 2010. Mechanical properties of wood. In: Wood handbook–wood as an engineering material. Ross, R., ed. General Technical Report FPL–GTR–190. Madison, WI: U.S. Department of Agriculture, Forest Service, Forest Products Laboratory: 5-1–5-46. Chapter 5.

Kulp, J.W. 1966. Report of Committee U-5, Post Service Records. Proceedings, Annual Meeting of the American Wood Preservers' Association. 64:18–88.

Laks, P.E.; Gutting, K.W.; Pickens, J.B.; DeGroot, R.C. 1996. Field performance of new wood preservative systems in secondary timber species. In: FPL-GTR-94. pp. 389-400. Madison, WI: U.S. Department of Agriculture, Forest Service, Forest Products Laboratory.

Lebow, S.T. 2010. Wood preservation. In: Wood handbook–wood as an engineering material. Ross, R., ed. General Technical Report FPL–GTR–190. Madison, WI: U.S. Department of Agriculture, Forest Service, Forest Products Laboratory: 15–1–15–28. Chapter 15.

Lebow, S.T.; C.A. Hatfield; S.A. Halverson. 2006. Effect of source, drying method and treatment schedule on treatability of red pine. Proceedings, 102nd Annual Meeting of the American Wood Preservers' Association. Austin, Texas, April 9–11, 2006. American Wood Protection Association, Birmingham, AL. 102:39–43.

Lebow, S.T.; Woodward, B.M.; Halverson, S.A.; Arango, R. 2010. Stake tests of northeastern species treated with copper-based preservatives: Five-year results. Research Note FPL–RN–0314. Madison, WI: U.S. Department of Agriculture, Forest Service, Forest Products Laboratory. 17 p.

Lebow, S.T.; Halverson, S.A.; Hatfield, C.A. 2005b. Treatability of underutilized northeastern species with CCA and alternative wood preservatives. Research Note FPL–RN–0300. Madison, WI: U.S. Department of Agriculture, Forest Service, Forest Products Laboratory. 5 p.

Lebow, S.T.; Hatfield, C.A.; Abbott, W. 2005a. Treatability of SPF framing lumber with CCA and borate preservatives. Wood and Fiber Science. 37(4):605–614.

Legault, R.A.; Preban, A.G. 1975. Kinetics of the atmospheric corrosion of low-alloy steels in an industrial environment, Corrosion. 31:117–122.

MacDonald, G.B. 1915. Preservative treatment of fence posts. Bulletin No. 158. Agricultural Experiment Station, Iowa State College Agriculture and Mechanics Arts. Ames, IA. 153 p.

Mackes, K.H.; D.L. Lynch. 2001. The effect of aspen wood characteristics and properties on utilization. In: Shepperd, W.D.; Binkley, D.; Bartos, D.L.; Stohlgren, T.J.; Eskew, L.G., comps. Sustaining aspen in western landscapes: Symposium proceedings. 13–15 June 2000; Grand Junction, CO. Proceedings RMRS-P-18. Fort Collins, CO: U.S. Department of Agriculture, Forest Service, Rocky Mountain Research Station. p. 429–440.

Markstrom, D.C.; Gjovik, L.R. 1992. Service life of treated and untreated Black Hills ponderosa pine fenceposts. Research paper RM–300. Fort Collins, CO: U.S. Department of Agriculture, Forest Service, Rocky Mountain Forest and Range Experiment Station: 9 p.

Matsukawa,Y.; Chuta, H.; Miyashita, M.; Yoshikawa, M.; Miyata, Y.; Asakura, S. 2011. Galvanic series of metals conventionally used in tap water with and without flow and its comparison to that in seawater. Corrosion. 67:125004–125007.

McIntyre, C.R. 2010. Comparison of micronized copper particle sizes and treatment of refractory species. Proceedings, 106th Annual Meeting of the American Wood Protection Association. May 23–25, 2010, Savannah, GA. 105:91–98.

MDOT. 2012. 2012 Standard specifications for construction. Supplemental Specification for Errata to the 2012 Standard Specifications. Michigan Department of Transportation. http://mdotcf.state.mi.us/public/specbook/2012/

MODOT, 2011. 2011 Specification book for highway construction. Section 1050, Lumber, Timber, Piling Posts and Poles. Missouri Department of Transportation. http://www.modot.org/business/standards_and_specs/highwayspecs.htm

Morrell, J.J; Miller, D.M.; Lebow, S.T. 1999. Above ground performance of preservative-treated western wood species. Proceedings, 94th Annual Meeting of the American Wood Preservers' Association. May 17–19, 1998, Scottsdale, AZ. 94(1):249–256.

Morrell, J.J.; Miller, D.J.; Schneider, P.F. 1999. Service life of treated and untreated fences posts: 1996 Post Farm report. Research Contribution 26, Forest Research Laboratory, Oregon State University. 24 p.

Morris, P.I.; Ingram, J.K. 2010. Field testing of wood preservatives XIX: Industrial preservatives. Proceedings, Annual Meeting of the Canadian Wood Preservation Association. 31:72–78.

Rammer, D.R.; Zelinka, S.L. 2008. Analytical determination of the surface area of a threaded fastener. ASTM Journal of Testing and Evaluation. 36:80–88.

Rammer, D.R. 2010. Fastenings. In: Wood handbook—wood as an engineering material. Ross, R., ed. General Technical Report, FPL–GTR–190. Madison, WI: U.S. Department of Agriculture, Forest Service, Forest Products Laboratory: 8-1-8-28. Chapter 8.

Rammer, D.R.; Zelinka, S.L. 2010. Optical method for measuring the surface area of a threaded fastener. Experimental Techniques. 34:36–39.

Richards, M.J.; McNamara, W.S. 1997. The field performance of CCA-C treated sawn refractory softwoods from North America. Document No. IRG/WP/40085. International Research Group on Wood Preservation. IRG Secretariat, Stockholm, Sweden. 26 p.

Richards, M.J.; Inwards, R.D. 1989. Treatability with CCA and initiation of field performance testing of refractory softwoods. Proceedings of the Canadian Wood Preservation Association. 10:144–178.

Simpson Strong-Tie. 2008. Preservative treated wood. Simpson Strong-Tie Technical Bulletin. T-PTWOODD08-R. Pleasanton, CA: Simpson Strong-Tie Company, Inc. 4 p.

Schmulsky, R. 2006. Dimensional stabilization of pine four-by-fours via restraint drying. Forest Products Journal. 56(3):41–43.

Simpson, W.T. 1991. Dry kiln operator's manual. Agricul-tural Handbook 188. United States Department of Agriculture, Forest Service, Forest Products Laboratory, Madison, WI. 274 p.

Slahor, J.J.; Hassler, C.C.; Dawson-Andoh, B. 2001. The durability of yellow-poplar and red-maple treated with ACQ-B. Forest Products Journal. 51(9):59–62.

Smith, W.B. 1986. Treatability of several northeastern species with chromated copper arsenate wood preservative. Forest Products Journal. 36(78):63–69.

Teesdale, C.H.; MacLean, J.D. 1918. Relative resistance of various hardwoods to injection with creosote. USDA For. Serv. Bulletin No. 606. Washington, DC. 36 p.

Tesoro, F.O., Choong, E.T.; Skarr, C. 1966. Transverse air permeability as an indicator of treatability with creosote. Forest Products Journal. 16(3):57–59.

Tsunoda, K. 1990. Laboratory evaluation of chemicals as wood preservatives. (1) 2- (Thiocyanomethylthio) benzo-thiazole (TCMTB). Wood Research. 77:28–34.

Webb, D.; Fox, R.; Pfeiffer, R.. 2010. Creosote posts–final inspection of the 1958 cooperative test after 50 years of exposure as a ground contact preservative. Proceedings, 105th Annual Meeting of the American Wood Protection Association. April 19–21, 2009, San Antonio, TX, 105:182–187.

Wengert, E.M.; Donnelly, D.M.; Markstrom, D.C.; Worth, H. E. 1985. Wood utilization. In: Debyle, N.V. and R.P. Winokur, eds. Aspen: ecology and management in the Western United States. USDA Forest Service, General Technical Report RM–119. Rocky Mountain Forest and Range Experiment Station. 283 p.

Wilson, J. 2004. Aluminum sign corrosion investigation. Final Report #WI-06-04 WisDOT Highway Research Study #WI-04-02, Madison, WI: Wisconsin Department of Transportation.

Wisconsin DNR. 2012. Wisconsin forest resources annual report. Madison, WI: Wisconsin Department of Natural Resources. http://dnr.wi.gov/topic/ForestBusinesses/documents/WisconsinForestResources.pdf

WisDOT. 2014. Transportation at a glance. Madison, WI: Wisconsin Department of Transportation. http://www.dot.wisconsin.gov/about/overview/glance.htm

Woodward, B.M.; Hatfield, C.A.; Lebow, S.T. 2011. Comparison of wood preservatives in stake tests: 2011 progress report. Research Note FPL–RN–02. Madison, WI: U.S. Department of Agriculture, Forest Service, Forest Products Laboratory. 120 p.

WSJ. 2012. Madison officials hope to make better use of trees expected to die from pest. Wisconsin State Journal, Nov. 3, 2012. http://host.madison.com/wsj/news/local/environment/madison-officials-hope-to-make-better-use-of-trees-expected/article_add7a614-2539-11e2-bbc5-001a4bcf887a html

Zelinka, S.; Derome, D.; Glass, S.V. 2011. Combining a hygrothermal and corrosion model to predict corrosion of metal fasteners embedded in wood. Building and Environment. 46:2060–2068.

Zelinka, S.L.; Rammer, D.R. 2009. Corrosion rates of fasteners in treated wood exposed to 100% relative humidity. ASCE Journal of Materials in Civil Engineering. 21: 758–763.

Zelinka, S.L.; Stone, D.S. 2011. Corrosion of metals in wood: Comparing the results of a rapid test method with long-term exposure tests across six wood treatments. Corrosion Science. 53:1708–1714.

Zelinka, S.L. 2007. Uncertainties in corrosion rate measurements of fasteners exposed to treated wood at 100% relative humidity. ASTM Journal of Testing and Evaluation. 35:106–109.

Zelinka, S.L.; Sichel, R.J.; Stone, D.S. 2010. Exposure testing of fasteners in preservative treated wood: gravimetric corrosion rates and corrosion product analyses. Corrosion Science. 52:3943–3948.

Zhang X.G.; Hwang, J.; Wu, W.K. 1998. Corrosion testing of steel and zinc. In: 4th International Conference on Zinc and Zinc Alloy Coated Steel Sheet: GALVATECH '98, Chiba, Japan.

Zhang, X.G. 2003. Corrosion of zinc and zinc alloys. In: S.D. Cramer, B.S. Covino (Eds.), ASM International, Materials Park, OH. pp. 402–417.

www.ingramcontent.com/pod-product-compliance
Lightning Source LLC
Chambersburg PA
CBHW080617290526
45790CB00007B/2819